TOP
GUN

FINANCIAL
SALES

TOP GUN

FINANCIAL
SALES

How to
Double or Triple
Your Results
While Reducing
Your Book

D. Scott Kimball

Dearborn™
Trade Publishing
A **Kaplan Professional** Company

Vice President and Publisher: Cynthia A. Zigmund
Editorial Director: Donald J. Hull
Senior Project Editor: Trey Thoelcke
Interior Design: Lucy Jenkins
Cover Design: Jody Billert
Typesetting: Elizabeth Pitts

Published by Dearborn Trade Publishing, a Kaplan Professional Company

Printed in the United States of America

03 04 05 10 9 8 7 6 5 4 3 2 1

Library of Congress Cataloging-in-Publication Data

Kimball, D. Scott.
    Top gun financial sales : how to double or triple your results while reducing your book / D. Scott Kimball.
        p.   cm.
Includes bibliographical references and index.
    ISBN 0-7931-6064-2
    1. Financial planners—Marketing. 2. Investment advisors—Marketing.
3. Success in business.
I. Title.
    HG179.5 .K55 2003
    332.6′068′8—dc21

2002014169

Dedicated to those with the courage to embrace change

CONTENTS

Thank you to Frank Rimkus, a Top Gun salesperson and my mentor on Wall Street. Frank gave me the "keys to the kingdom" by letting me learn at his side. To "the Reverend" George J. Carter, who was one of the best salespeople and motivators I've ever seen. George, you inspired me and showed me what it meant to perform at levels most people cannot even imagine. To Gordy and Vinnie, there is a special place in heaven for you two guys. To Mike Velasco, a Top Gun Producer who embraced the Top Gun Model and is a daily living testament to how well it can work. Thank you to Catherine Harris, a truly gifted writer, who encouraged me to continue to write and was instrumental in pushing this book across the finish line. To Don Hull and the Top Gun team at Dearborn Trade Publishing . . . it has only been my pleasure to work with your team of professionals. To my parents, who believe that the most important thing you can give a child is self-confidence. To my wife, Teri, who has always been my biggest fan, best friend, and most trusted critic. Thank you to the hundreds of professional brokers, financial consultants, financial planners and advisors, investment bankers, salespeople, analysts, CEOs, CFOs, Treasurers, hedge fund managers, managers, clients, sales executives, interns, sales assistants, wire room operators—you have woven a vivid and exciting life for me. You are the reason I love Wall Street. Finally, thank you to the Toronto Blue Jays, who released me from my player contract many years ago, which allowed me to find a passion other than baseball . . . Wall Street.

As a young adviser in California many years ago, I cold called a man named Bob. Despite my youth, he agreed to see me and talk about his money. I was so green I didn't even know what he did for a living. When I visited his posh offices, there really wasn't anything there to overtly indicate the source of his wealth. So I just asked. He smiled broadly and said, "I make thousands of people smile every day. It's the greatest job on earth. I sell ice cream." What made him different than the boy who works down at the local ice cream parlor is that Bob sold *a lot* of ice cream through hundreds of locations. I'll never forget that day. It was the first time I really ever associated "work" with fun and happiness. Work, to me, had always been something people had to do so they could have fun and be happy when they got *home* from work. But this man was genuinely happy doing his job and, quite obviously, he had done it very well.

I was in my early 20s, Bob in his 50s. I didn't have a dime to my name, Bob had many millions. Yet he spent a day walking, talking, and sailing with me. He showed me, through his example that someone can be happy, fun-loving, committed to his and her family, and an all around decent human being as well as a wealthy and successful businessperson. I decided then and there—without even being aware of it—that I would strive to be the kind of man that Bob was. I don't think he ever knew the kind of impact he made on me, but I will never forget him.

Today, as I survey my own life, I realize I *have* achieved many of the same things that Bob had when I met him. I'm happily married, have three great kids, I'm successful in my career, and I love what I do every day. I've often wondered how I can ever thank Bob for the positive way he influenced my life, and I realize I can't. There is no way I can pay him back. So, therefore, I've decided to pass the message on. It is my intention to show as many people as I can that being successful in life is within all of our grasps.

At the time I created the Top Gun Sales business model, the concepts and thinking that are central to Top Gun went directly against years of teaching and training by the largest firms on Wall Street. Some time after I released the first edition of this book, *Registered Rep* magazine, an industry magazine for financial planners and brokers, ran a story about how one firm had put forth an initiative for a new business model dubbed "SuperNova." Although I know little about SuperNova, I've been told that some of the concepts behind it are similar and complimentary to those outlined in this book. I think this is great. It validates what I've been saying for years. Much of the financial industry seems to be getting it right—or at least my perception of right. Financial advisors at UBS, PaineWebber, Merrill Lynch, Morgan Stanley, Raymond James, Deutsche Banc Alex. Brown, and Bank of America are using the Top Gun model in some form or fashion or have adopted some of the principles of Top Gun Financial Sales.

Of all the people I've spoken to and all the people who have been early adopters of the Top Gun Model, one man stands out, however. His name is Michael. Michael was an excellent producer before we ever met. When he heard me speaking to a group about the Top Gun Model, he listened. It made sense to him. He told me afterwards that he was going to do it. I asked, "Do what?" He said, "Everything you just said. I'm going to do it." Not many people are willing to give themselves and their businesses over to something new. But this made sense to him. He said he saw the simple elegance of the Top Gun Model, and he was looking for a better way to work.

I could see Michael was serious. I encouraged him to call me as often as he needed to and to let me know how it was going. About eight months later I received an e-mail, outlining a transaction that had occurred at Michael's firm. The firm was very proud of this transaction and the broker who handled it. This broker was going to receive a commission of $3.3 million. I'm sure you've guessed—the broker was Michael—and he credited the Top Gun Model for getting him focused on what was important in his business and eventually leading him to that big payday (there were more to follow).

What's interesting about this story is that Michael didn't need a new way of working his business. He would have been considered a top producer at any firm in the country before he ever met me or heard about Top Gun. But, with an open mind and a lack of ego, he was eager to explore an avenue that could even further his already staggering success. My point is: If you're sitting there reading this and thinking that it doesn't really apply to you because you're already a top producer at your firm, you might want to think again. You see, Michael was a top producer before adopting the Top Gun Model. He's now one of the most elite financial sales producers in the country. There are only a handful of people in his league.

Our business is changing constantly. It's always been a changing business; it *has* to change to keep up with the trends. But, with everything that has gone on in our country recently, we're seeing changes happen at a much faster pace. Many firms have decided to focus on the High Net Worth clientele and devote their efforts and resources to this wealthier segment of the market. They also seem to be letting go of many brokers who aren't doing fee-based business or who aren't catering to this elite clientele. Sales forces are shrinking. Prudential was in the news recently, rumored to be ousting all brokers who don't produce more than $325,000 annually. Deutsche Bank is closing and selling offices, taking their brokerage force down in number, and talking about only servicing the "Ultra High Net Worth." Wall Street is indeed changing, and it seems to be embracing the broker who can do over $1 million in gross fees or commissions annually. That is the new benchmark. Branch managers have been told not to even consider hiring people who do less. No more trainees—producers only.

For now it appears that if you want to stay in this business, you better get to the magic number, and do it quickly. Top Gun is all about performing at the highest levels and getting you to substantially increase your production, no matter where you're starting. If you're a $500,000 producer, Top Gun is designed to take you to $1.5 million or higher. If you're a million-dollar producer, Top Gun can get you to $3 million or $4 million. The Top Gun method requires you to be realistic about your own strengths and weaknesses and also about your firm's strengths and weaknesses. You will need to take responsibility for where you are now and commit to where you will be in six months and six years. With the Top Gun method I can help you get to that point of mental clarity where you are no longer confused about what to do next in your financial career. When you get rid of the clutter, thinking clearly and optimistically is easy.

It never made sense to me that in order to do well in financial sales you had to have 2,000 clients, but that's what they taught us at all the big firms a few years ago. So, I did it the way they taught and it made my life miserable. I always felt you could never truly do a good job for *any* client if you had too many clients to service. The solution came to me very clearly. If I had 50 *great* clients, I could give far better service to those 50 clients than if I continued to try to service every client who wanted to invest any amount of money. Don't get me wrong. Everybody is entitled to invest his or her money, no matter what the amount. But, I had already spent several years on small accounts. It was time to get serious.

I had just spent five years gathering as many accounts as possible, had been working my ass off, and had been in the top quintile of my sales class every year. Yet, with all that work and all that money under management, I was miserable. I hated my life. I weighed 275 pounds, and my kids had to beg me to get up and go to work. After conceiving and implementing the Top Gun Model, my gross sales declined the next year, but the momentum was building and I could feel it. Things were happening. It was working. Refusing to become discouraged, I stuck with it. The following year was the breakout year. I did over $1 million in production. The year after, I increased that amount by nearly 20 percent. Every year since has shown amazing growth. My assets grew well into the nine figures, and my personal production kept running up into the seven figures. How is this possible? The secret lies in the Top Gun Model.

During some of the most disastrous financial times in history and in the space of a few short years, my production tripled using the system outlined on the pages before you.

This book is written for the person who seeks to perform at a very high level. It's for the person who has decided that living life as an average producer is no longer acceptable. The Top Gun producers in the world do $10 million, $20 million, $30 million in sales. Some of them have built support teams around them; some of them are still doing it alone. If you want to get to the level where you are doing truly extraordinary numbers, it will take more *effort,* but probably less *work* than you imagine. Half of what you need is mental and the other half is consistency. I call it doing "pushups" every day.

Not long ago I was working endless hours and not making nearly enough money. That's all changed now. I have a great quality of life, and I want that for you, too. *That's* why I wrote this book. It's designed to be a short, easy-to-understand read, something you can take with you to study on the plane, train, or standing in line. If you implement the Top Gun Model, I submit it is almost impossible *not* to see your business increase. And the ancillary benefits of having entered into this way of working your business are even more rewarding than money. You'll have more time for your family and will feel better about the job you are doing for your clients—because you *will* be doing a better job.

If, however, you are perfectly content and feel you know all you need to know about selling in the financial services business, then put this book down so someone with a burning desire to succeed can pick it up and buy it.

CHAPTER ONE

PERFORMANCE

Performance, and performance alone,
dictates the predator in any food chain.

NAVY SEAL TEAM SAYING

Your destiny is not a matter of chance,
it's a matter of choice.

WILLIAM JENNINGS BRYAN

In 1969, a few U.S. Navy fighter pilots began the Advanced Fighter Weapons Training School known today as Top Gun. Our pilots were still "downing" two planes to each one of ours we lost, but this was still not what we were accustomed to. In response to the dramatic drop in the "kill ratio" over the skies of Vietnam, Top Gun was formed in order to teach air-to-air combat strategy and tactics to the best pilots in each squadron. U.S. pilots were sustaining heavy losses, being outmaneuvered by smaller, faster aircraft. The U.S. planes had some distinct disadvantages, but they also had some advantages. The objective of Top Gun was to raise the kill ratio. In order to accomplish that goal, they focused on two things:

1. Assess and maximize the effectiveness of the tools at their disposal.

1

2. Teach combat strategy and tactics that would allow them to vastly outperform the enemy with the tools they had today.

The results of the Top Gun school were dramatic. The kill ratio in 1969 at the beginning of the Top Gun school was 2:1. The U.S. shot down two planes for every one of ours that fell. By the end of the war, the kill ratio was 12:1, and in the last 8 months or so of the conflict, the U.S. pilots were running a kill ratio of 21:1. The pilots gave credit for their success to what they learned at the Top Gun school.

In business, and in sales in particular, we can apply the same methods used at the U.S. Navy's Top Gun. We can assess the weapons we have at our companies—known as products and services—review our individual business models, learn strategic and tactical methods to win business from the competition, and endeavor to perform at levels far beyond average. The Top Gun Model is designed to provide you with the process, the strategies, and the tactics to perform at levels usually never reached by the average person in your industry.

Batting Practice and Pushups

In *High Performance Selling*, Terry Beck talks about the successful salespeople he has known and what makes them that way. He notes that although they can come in all shapes and sizes, can have a negative or positive outlook on life, and can be different in many other ways, there are two distinguishing traits that set them apart: (1) Successful salespeople make things happen for themselves, and (2) they never give up.

In that way, he says, top performing salespeople are much like baseball players. A good baseball player will fail seven out of the ten times that he goes up to the plate to hit. Yet he still goes up there every time with the belief that in this at bat, he will hit. Not hitting is simply an option that never enters his mind. Some people would say that given the facts and the statistics, this makes him stupid. I think it makes him a winner.

I have some personal knowledge in this area. Before I got into the business of financial sales, I was a pro baseball player for the Toronto Blue Jays. I wasn't particularly gifted, but I worked hard and was able to fulfill my childhood dream. I played for and against and lived with some of the best. Players like Pat Borders, Cecil Feilder, Jimmy Key, Vince Coleman, David Wells, Ricky Henderson, "Bip" Roberts, Freddy "Crime Dog" McGriff, and many others. As naturally talented as these guys are, they knew that in order to be the best and stay the best, they needed to work on their game. They took batting practice every day. Every day they worked on perfecting the great swings they had *and* trying new ones. Keeping their games as good as they were wasn't enough. They continually looked for ways to improve themselves.

In the sales business, "taking batting practice" or "doing your pushups" means contacting new people. You've got to do it every day. Winning teams take batting practice and do their pushups *every day*. If you don't contact new people every day, you'll lose your edge. If you lose your edge, my team will start to beat your team. My team will take your best clients away from you because they've practiced, put in the time, and are prepared. We will be relentless. Once we take one client away from you, we're going to find out how we can better serve others and "run up the score." If we steal a single base from you, we won't stop running until you throw us out. Once we've identified a weakness in your business or methodology, we're going to exploit it. In tough times, when the market for new accounts isn't growing—in fact—is probably declining, how do we grow our business? Like any other business—by taking market share away from weaker competitors. My goal is to get all your best clients and make you look for a job at McDonalds.

My sales team takes batting practice every day. We're on the phone calling new people and meeting them in person (Some of them could be your clients!), making our presentations. Each member of our team contacts at least ten new people a day. We play offense—and we're going to put you on defense. And we will win . . . because we are the best. At least, that's our mindset. If you want to stay alive in this business, you better learn how to compete with me—because before I die I intend to give McDonalds a whole bunch of overqualified management trainees.

Now, in order to win business from you, we have to provide something you don't. What we provide is performance, by delivering a better process, a better methodology, and better service. In the end, the customers have to believe they will have more of what they want by doing business with us than by doing business with you. We have our personal strengths, and we have a set of proprietary weapons and natural strengths at our disposal—given to us by our firm. How we arrange them, deploy them, price them, and ultimately fire them at you will determine who wins the account. You may have had better performance last year than we did, you may have better tools today, but you will not execute or use the tools you have with the same degree of intelligence or consistency that we use ours. Nor will you service the client the same way we will. We're Top Gun. Ultimately, we believe we will outperform you on more than one front. That is why we will ultimately win the business.

I'm exaggerating here for effect, of course . . . sort of. We're in a business that is humbling, even to the best, and remaining humble is important. But that doesn't mean you cannot be proud of who you are and what you do well. You need to have the level of confidence I just depicted in order to win in this business. You've got to get better at what you do or someone will come along and ruin your day. Believe me, no one is interested in taking the clients you don't care about. Your competitors are going after the two or three or ten clients that make up the majority of your revenue. They will gladly leave you the rest. You've got to stay ahead of the competition. You have to be better.

In sales of any kind, performance is everything. Whether you manage money, sell services, or manage people on Wall Street, our economic system is designed to reward performance and weed out the weak. As the Navy SEAL quotation alludes to in the epigraph that opens this chapter, performance does dictate the predator in any food chain. Think about it. In business, the stronger companies devour or crush the weaker companies. Performance counts. It matters. Extraordinary performers in our business are paid extraordinarily well. Nonperformers are shown the door. In the world of sports, medicine, arts, music, and business, the exceptional performers make huge amounts of money and are able to influence the world around them. They can have impact. They can influence and shape lives. The same is true for you and me in the business of financial sales. We have to do our pushups every day. Our pushups are cold calls. Batting practice for you and me is contacting ten new people every day.

It's a special person who can step up to the plate every day and truly believe down to the soles of his or her feet that a sale will be made on every call. Maybe it's the knowledge that like in baseball, where you can win the World Series with just one hit, landing that one amazing account can be life changing. Whatever it is, being in the top 10 percent of your firm makes your contribution substantial. It puts you among the elite. If you are already producing in the top 10 percent of your firm, perhaps it's time to look at how you can get into the top 10 percent of the United States—or in the profession worldwide. Why not keep trying to improve? Staying complacent is not a good thing.

The Top Gun Model is a set of guidelines, rules, and strategies designed to streamline a financial service professional's business. The structure is designed for efficiency, balance, high productivity, high profitability, low risk, and a focus on revenue production. The goal is to simplify your life while at the same time increasing your income. Rather than dictate exactly what kind of business you should do, I present an open architecture for the Top Gun Model, leaving it up to you to design a specific Top Gun business based upon your own areas of expertise, your natural client base, and the strengths of your firm.

What I've tried to do is give you a practical methodology for becoming a Top Gun producer with the assumption that you are interested in producing "out of the box" results for your business by adopting Top Gun producer strategies and tactics. I expect you will finish this book with a business model that is measurable, efficient, and highly profitable to you and your firm. I want people to look at your business growth a year or so from now and ask, "How are you doing this? What's going on here?" You'll know you're on the right track if your peers are convinced that you're getting special treatment of some kind from management.

The Top Gun Model isn't for everybody. Not everybody wants to be in the top 10 percent of their business, and the Top Gun Model isn't the only way to get there. But for many of us, what is in this book makes sense. It's not complex, nor does it conform to any particular "firm strategy." You and I will create it together. It is *our* strategy, *our* model, *our* way of doing business, . . . a way that is simpler, more efficient, more productive, and more profitable than models that have been forced upon us in the past. Those models are no longer valid. The Top Gun Model allows you to make changes that will have impact on your business in any kind of market environment. Hopefully it will be the last model you will ever need.

When the Navy pilots formed the Top Gun school in 1969, they did it for themselves; they did it because their "boss," the U.S. government, was not going to give them different planes to fly. They had a choice. Either they figured out how to fight more efficiently with what they had or be killed by the enemy. It's quite the same for us today. However difficult a state our economy might be in, however crazy the stock market might be behaving, it is the same market for every broker in the United States. We've got to figure out a way to make it work for ourselves. The Top Gun broker will find a way to make it work *very well.*

Let's be honest here. Our firms don't care if we, personally, make them money. They just want *someone* to make them money. If we fail, there's always another broker ready to step into our seat. But *we* care. Our families care. The Top Gun program is dedicated to you and me. We're the people in the trenches doing the work. This is our model. I've had great success using it. For the elite financial salespeople, there's plenty of money out there—more than enough for you *and* me to have success stories. If you do better by using the Top Gun Model, then we'll both be successful.

Naturally, you're not going to be transformed into a Top Gun salesperson by reading this book alone. This isn't magic, it's a technique, . . . a way for *you to work* more effectively. Most people know what it takes to succeed in whatever it is they do for a living. Only a few actually do it. It's all about consistent performance. A natural level of talent is helpful. Unfortunately, nobody comes into a career with experience. We all have to put in the time, we all have to learn our trade. Knowledge cannot be faked. Many people have tried to prove otherwise, but it doesn't work. You've got to know what you're talking about. You may be able to fool a few, but sooner or later you'll get caught if you try to pretend you know more than you do. My recommendation is not to try. Take the time. Learn your trade. As important as knowledge *is,* a burning desire and a passion for what you do is equally as significant to your success. Elite performance is a combination of talent, knowledge, passion, and consistency.

Elite performers make it look easy. But they only make it look easy because they have a burning desire to succeed and they "grind it out" every day, doing their pushups, rehearsing their pitches, striving every day to win.

I experienced this vividly in the summer of 2001. I was in Las Vegas on business and went to see a friend one day in between meetings. We were driving from his house to lunch at a country club and as we passed the practice tee, he pointed to the lone figure on the tee. "Recognize that guy?" he asked. It was Tiger Woods. It was 103 degrees outside, and Tiger was on the tee practicing. We watched for a while as he methodically worked on his irons, then we drove on. We went to lunch, and my friend asked me to come back up to his house after I was done with my meetings so we could grill some steaks and talk some more. As I drove back up to his house at dusk, Tiger was still there. I couldn't believe it. I told my friend, and he said, "Yeah. He does that all the time. He'll be there until dark."

That's what I'm talking about.

CHAPTER TWO

THE NINE REASONS FOR FAILURE

Men do not attract that which they want,
but that which they are.

JAMES ALLEN

There are nine major reasons for failure in financial sales. Of course there are man y more than that, but these nine show themselves time and time again and really seem to be stumbling blocks for financial advisers in pursuit of greatness.

Unknown Mission

The first reason for failure is lack of planning. You see, stockbrokers are people who are part businessperson, part artist. Left and right brain people rolled into one. As a result, many of us don't formulate a plan, process, or strategy for accomplishing our goals. This is something a person who is all business would see as essential, but an artist sees it as boring and possibly inhibiting to the practice of his art. Do you know where you're taking your career? Or are you letting your career take *you,* hoping a few lucky breaks will get you in the big leagues? You've got to *know* where you're going if you want to be a Top Gun. No one is *that* lucky. No one ever made it to the top and stayed there by accident. Be a professional. Think about where you're going and how you're going to get there.

Lesson: *Know your mission.*

No Clear Niche

The second reason for failure is that many people in this business try to be too many things to too many people. We chase down as many clients as we possibly can, tell them we can help them no matter what they need, and hope for the best. Nobody is an expert at everything, and nobody has to be. What successful businessperson do you know that doesn't know his and her market niche? The top producers in our field have focused in on one or two areas and have made them their specialty. They know their areas of expertise as well or better than anyone else in the business. While they may be familiar with other parts of the business, they don't pretend to be experts in areas where they are not. We provide a service. You don't get to be number one by providing lousy service. Have you ever said to a client, "I can give you some basic information about that, but I'd like to refer you to an associate of mine who knows more about this part of the business than anyone else"? If you were the client, wouldn't you appreciate that kind of honesty? When it comes to people's money, they want the best information available. Know what you do best and know who is the best at other parts of the business. You'll not only develop better relationships with your clients, but you'll develop lasting and profitable relationships with your associates.

Lesson: Develop expertise and find a niche.

Owning Your Results

Third on the list of reasons for failure is our failure to take responsibility for our performance and our circumstances. Unfortunately, it is becoming more and more prevalent to blame others or events for our lot in life. The market is difficult, my boss doesn't like me, the other reps get special treatment, I don't come from the right family, I didn't go to the right school. All just excuses for our failures, but nothing that will get us from our current place to a better place. In the end, no matter how many excuses you use or other people you wish to blame, you end up owning your results, your place in life, your performance, good or bad. We are all clearly the result of the sum total of the decisions and choices we have made.

Lesson: You are exactly where you are because of the cumulative effect of the decisions you, and you alone, have made.

Unwilling to Make Changes

Fourth, we are unwilling to make the changes necessary to create the business we say we desire. Unwillingness to change seems to be a normal human condition for most people, so it's not abnormal to want to keep things the way they are. Failing to change will, however, kill you in this business. According to Gayle Davis, PhD, author of *High Performance Thinking for Business, Sports, and Life*, ". . . when you work on change and feel uncomfortable, strange, awkward, you know you are moving toward accomplishing your goal because you are out of your comfort zone." In order to be successful in sales, you cannot be comfortable. It's fine to be confident with your process, your methodology, the firm you work for, and the products you sell. But being confident and comfortable are two different things. Getting too comfortable is getting complacent. As soon as you do that, someone is going to clean your clock. Picture a Navy SEAL sitting in a jungle with his face camouflaged, his gun across his lap, silence all around. Do you think he's saying to himself, "Gee, this is sure a beautiful jungle, and so peaceful. I think I'll just shut my eyes and enjoy the surroundings." No. He's on high alert all the time, his head is moving side to side, and his eyes are wide open, until he's home safely. That's how you need to be from the minute you step in the office to the minute you get home.

Lesson: *Be willing to make changes.*

Not Knowing What You Do

Our fifth mistake is that we are often confused about who we are and what we do. We are salespeople. A lot of people think they are something else in this business such as money managers, hedge fund managers, day traders, analysts, investment bankers, but they aren't. We are salespeople. We sell. That's what we have to focus on. High performance and focus go hand in hand. Let other people focus on managing money, trading, and analyzing. Hire an analyst yourself. Hire or outsource everything except selling. Because selling is our job and it's what we should do best. You may wish to portray yourself as an investment consultant or advisor or analyst for marketing purposes. There's really nothing wrong with that, but people who start to believe their own press are usually headed for a rude awakening. Remember who you are and what you do best.

Lesson: Don't be confused about who you really are . . . you're a salesperson. You SELL.

Not Making Heroes Out of Your Clients

The sixth reason for failure—and this is important—is that we are too often concerned more with what the clients could do for us rather than with what we can do for our clients. It is our job to make them heroes. This is such an easy thing to say but is not often put into practice. Imagine what the world would be like if people in the service business actually devoted their daily efforts to serving. There are some organizations that do just this, one of my favorites being the Ritz-Carlton. I love staying there. In fact, I love being around most any of their hotels. Why? Because everyone you come in contact with at the Ritz-Carlton is working 24/7, running in double time to make their guests happy. This is their mission, and they execute their mission every day. They have separated themselves from the competition. Recently, I had a client fly in from out of town. He called from the airport, sounding distracted. When I asked him what was wrong, he said he stupidly left his telephone charger at home and his cell phone battery was just about to run out. Because he was running late, he asked me to call the Ritz-Carlton and tell them that he was indeed on his way. I did just that, explaining about his cell phone and lack of charger. The concierge told me everything would be taken care of. When my client arrived, the charger he needed was waiting for him in the room with a note from *me*. The Ritz-Carlton made me look like a hero to my client. They didn't take credit for what happened—their concern was making me look good. The Ritz is not confused! This is what you need to do. Making heroes of your clients to the people they have to please should be your mission. When you do that, you will have succeeded in making this person a client for life.

Lesson: *Make heroes of your clients.*

You Stopped Prospecting

Number seven is, we stop prospecting. We get a few bucks in the bank, we get a nice title, we think we've become too busy or too important. This is such ego crap. This is like being a professional baseball player and not taking batting practice. It won't be long before you start striking out. Prospecting, cold calling, networking, whatever you do to earn new business, keeps you sharp. Sharpens your pencil. It keeps you in touch with the market and, possibly, what your very own clients may be thinking and not telling you. Prospecting is not beneath any of us, it's smart business. As I've said earlier, I call it "doing my pushups." You have to do your pushups every day if you want your chest and arms to be strong. How many do you do every day? 15? 20? 50? If you do just 10 prospecting "pushups" every day, you're probably doing 10 more than almost everyone in the business. Your financial results will reveal it—just the way your chest and arms do.

Lesson: *Never, never, never stop prospecting.*

You Waste Time

Our eighth greatest reason for failure is that we aren't efficient. It is a known fact that salespeople across all the country (in *any* business) spend approximately 33 percent of their working time talking to high probability prospects. Only 33 percent! That means the other 67 percent of the time we are talking to people who don't need or want our services, don't know what we do, or don't have any money to invest. What is *that* all about?

Lesson: *Don't waste time talking to people who do not further your mission.*

Lack of Execution

The final reason for failure in our business (and just about anything else you can fail at in life) is lack of consistency. The reason so many Top Gun brokers are willing to tell you "how they do it" is because they have figured out that there are no real secrets to success on the street . . . except that the differentiating factor, the "hinge factor," if you will, is in the *execution.* The daily, relentless, consistent, execution of their business plan over and over again, day in and day out. That is the only secret to success. They know that nine out of ten people cannot execute consistently. So why keep it a secret? As Dr. Davis writes in *High Performance Thinking for Business, Sports, and Life,* "It's not what you do occasionally that changes your life; its what you do consistently. At first, you make your habits. Then your habits make you." Doing your "pushups," reminding yourself of your mission, focusing on your niche, rehearsing your pitch . . . are all part of consistently executing. The team or person who executes every day will eventually beat the team that has more talent, family connections, the best tools, the better name, more money, etc. That in which you are consistent, tells the story of your life.

Lesson: Execution is everything. Execute every day.

Why are these nine lessons important? Because in order to rapidly ramp up your business, you need to know what land mines to step around and what mistakes to avoid. Other men and women have taught us these lessons, and to them we should be grateful. Some have sacrificed their careers. Others have sacrificed their incomes. Let us respect their teachings without following in their footsteps. I don't have time to learn *every* lesson the hard way, do you?

CHAPTER THREE

THE MODEL

I don't know the key to success,
but the key to failure
is trying to please everyone.

BILL COSBY

The goal of the Top Gun Model is to create a business that is highly productive, highly profitable, low maintenance, low risk, and scalable. It is all about consistent high performance. If you want to achieve this, you have to "buy into" the two principles that lie at the heart of The Top Gun Model.

Make Heroes Out of Others

It's not enough to figure out how to make your client happy. The real secret is in discovering who it is your *client* needs to make happy and helping him and her to do that. If you can figure out whose respect, praise, and admiration is important to your client and come up with a way to help make it happen, you will have a client for life. He and she will always find a way to do business with you.

I cannot stress enough the importance of making heroes of your clients. The Ritz-Carlton was our earlier example. Whatever effort you have to put out to do this will come back to you a hundredfold in the long run. Of this I am quite sure. One of my clients is an executive at a major firm. One afternoon we sat on his porch together while he told me about an acquisition his company had made recently and turned over to him. Unfortunately, this acquisition came with a big problem. I told him I thought this could be a good thing because if he could solve the problem, he'd be a hero.

For the next several hours we put our heads together and tried to figure out a solution while we planted in his yard. We talked about the business and all of its intricacies. Then I remembered a similar situation that happened at another company ten years before. I even surprised myself by remembering how they solved the problem. My client vaguely remembered it, too, as it had received quite a bit of publicity back then. The more we remembered about the case, the more we realized the two problems were, in fact, *very* similar. He used it as an example and case history to argue his solution to senior management, and they bought it. Of course, my client did a tremendous amount of work to get the problem solved, but our conversation pointed him in the right direction and helped him to crystallize his thinking. He became a hero and has never forgotten my willingness to work through the problem with him until he got on the right track. More important, he has referred me to at least ten new clients.

Here's another example. I have a client who is a treasurer of a corporation. I was thinking about his job, what he is required to do every day, and how I might help him become a hero at his company. In looking over his financial reports, I noticed that the company had an outstanding issue of convertible bonds trading for less than par. Interest rates had dropped quite a bit from the time the bonds were issued. Because this company does have cash, the opportunities are many in this scenario. I suggested a couple to him. He could buy back some of the bonds, thereby lowering his interest expense and "retiring" outstanding shares of stock for reporting purposes. This could potentially raise earnings per share. He could also do an interest rate swap, trading his high fixed rate for a much lower floating rate, thereby lowering interest expense. Either one of these ideas, when presented to his senior management team, would allow him to provide real opportunities for increasing earnings per share and structuring interest income and expense more profitably.

Once you help a client become a hero to those important to him, you become a confidante. He and she will figure out a way to pay you handsomely for your effort. You will become a member of his and her inner circle, and wherever that client goes in the future, so shall you follow.

Do High Margin, High Probability, Low Risk Business

Principle Number Two is that of Margin, Probability, and Risk, or MPR. Margin is a measurement of the profitability of a business. Costs, or expenses, lower profitability. In our business, two of the highest costs we incur are those of time and energy. If we have clients who take large amounts of our time and energy to acquire and maintain, but who don't pay us well, then they may be low margin. In other words, they don't allow us to spend our time on projects that are financially productive. We want high margin clients and we want to do high margin business with them.

Do High Margin, High Probability, Low Risk Business. *With MPR we align our actions with our desired results.* Doing this is the single most important goal you can have. *Align your actions with your desired results.* MPR is about allocating your most precious resource—your time—on tasks that produce high margin revenue and accomplish your goals. Are you talking to people about business that has the following characteristics: Higher Margins, Higher Probability, and Lower Risk? Are you consistently asking yourself if what you're doing has these three characteristics? If not, you can find yourself involved in lengthy discussions with people about financial matters that should have been well understood by the average Bubba before he graduated from the local city college. This is not business that will pay you well. It may be low risk, and you may have a high probability of closing the sale, but you won't be paid well for your time. Look for the business that has all three characteristics: Higher Margins, Higher Probability of Closing, and Lower Risk.

High Margin

The Top Gun Model doesn't have room for low margin clients. You need to have the bulk of your day, and your assistant's day, free to go after making real money for both your team and your clients. Searching for bigger, better, higher margin clients.

Helping your existing relationships make money and become bigger and better clients. Bringing a higher level of thinking to your existing clients, making heroes out of them to their superiors. If you have to spend three days on a project for a client that has no hope of earning you or the client a penny, you need to seriously question what you're doing. That's what other people do, not you. It may sound arrogant, but if a client who pays you nothing every year is asking you to go back over three years of statements to determine the cost basis of some fractional shares of a mutual fund that was purchased ages ago, then you have to ask yourself why. That's what bookkeepers do. Your firm has bookkeepers—assign that stuff to them. That is what *they* get paid for, not you.

Another example of a low margin client is one who deposits $50 million in a single stock with you, holding out the carrot that he or she will do more business with you—or give you the trade when the time comes. Somehow the time never seems to come for making the trade. That client certainly won't pay you a fee on the stock. These are the worst types of clients because they lead you on. They use you to get your best thinking, research, and expertise as it applies to the rest of their portfolio assets (which, by the way, they don't hold with you). They'll grind you on pricing and eventually do the trade with someone else. Even worse than the fact that you are unlikely to be paid a cent for all your effort, they waste your most precious asset— your time. If you don't structure your business to prevent this from happening, it will. You have to be able to recognize this type of client up-front and to have something in writing that requires him or her to enter into some sort of contractual agreement that pays you, beginning today.

A low margin client is also the one who is constantly giving you limit orders for stocks or bonds that have almost no hope of being executed, or who is constantly complaining about how much you get paid for what you do instead of focusing on how much he's making. These are negative, time wasting clients. Send them away. You have to be positively focused on making money for the clients who *do* appreciate you, and on looking for new business. You really want a limited number of clients who *love* what you do for them, trust you wholeheartedly, and who don't mind talking up your service and talent to others. Life is too short to do it any other way.

I had a client for whom I'd done a couple of favors by putting him in front of some of our firm's better offerings. He made good money in these special situations, which aren't available to everyone, only our best clients. On another day we did a trade for which he was charged a commission. He called to tell me he thought the commission was too high. I had to remind him about the favors I'd done for him over the last few months, favors that had earned him some nice money—money that I was not expected to earn him on situations I was by no means obligated to offer him. I just hate being put in this position by a client—don't you? I can't stand people who have to be reminded constantly of what you've done for them in order to justify your fees. To heck with them. Send them away.

I'd much rather spend my time with issues for clients like the couple I have in Missouri, John and Sue. John and Sue became clients many years ago, long before they retired. We hit it off right from the beginning, but we also had an exceptional working relationship. They knew I took their money very seriously. Not once in all the years I've been working with them did they ever mention how much I charged for my services. John and Sue trusted that if they paid me what I thought was fair, I would treat them well and do an exceptional job for them. They called me one day and said they were thinking about their retirement. They didn't need to retire just yet but wanted *me* to tell them when they could retire, and when that happened, how much I would feel comfortable delivering to them monthly without them running out of money.

What an honor, to be trusted with such important issues! They put the responsibility for their portfolio and retirement income in my hands. They let me tell them when they could retire. They let me tell them how much they can spend every month. I made all those decisions for them. That kind of trust deserves the utmost respect. I work my ass off for John and Sue, making sure their accounts are safe and that they are earning what they need to earn and that they get the best I have to offer every day, every week, and every month. I now own responsibility for their retirement.

For every client out there who wants to waste our time and lower our margin, there are clients like John and Sue, who make our jobs meaningful. So why do we waste our time working for people we don't like, who don't appreciate or trust us, and who constantly make us justify our value?

High Probability

The next part of MPR is High Probability. The fact is that 60 percent to 65 percent of most salespeople's time is spent on prospects that are low quality leads or will become very low margin clients—the kind of clients we wish we never had. What we want is to spend nearly 100 percent of our time talking to, or

27

presenting to people or corporations that have a high probability of becoming high margin, high paying, and low risk clients. So, how do you do that?

It's basically very simple. You leverage your time by having an assistant or associate prescreen your leads. That way, by the time you go to make the call or the presentation, you're working on a high probability of success. The time invested in teaching an assistant or associate how to identify potentially high margin clients is worth it. If you can't get an assistant or an associate to screen for you, then do the prescreening yourself during off-hours or on the weekends. There is no sense wasting your valuable time during the day chasing clients who have no intention of giving you their business, or, giving you business that you don't want.

Low Risk

The last part of the MPR equation is Low Risk. The risk involved in this business is what affords us the opportunity to earn a great deal of money. There are a lot of risky areas: market risk, client litigation risk, risk of failing to make the right investment decisions, risk of not producing enough to stay employed. Still, none of these risks are bigger than making the wrong choice of clients.

If you choose to do business with people who have little money, you won't make your production numbers and you will fail. If you choose to take any business you can get, you'll find yourself too busy to handle everyone well. You'll get complaints and possibly lawsuits. At the very least, you'll make mistakes, you'll neglect accounts, and you'll pay a price for that. If you choose to spend your time going after a low margin, highly saturated market—already effectively handled by the discounters and online firms—you will fail. If you choose to do business in an area in which your firm is weak and doesn't have a competitive edge simply because a potential client asks you to, your competition will eventually take the account.

Think about if for a minute. Every time you add a client to the firm, you take on risk for yourself and your firm. Don't you think it would behoove us to be as cautious as possible when choosing our clients? Ideally, you want to seek out clients who are reasonably risk-averse. You don't need clients who insist on putting their money at high risk. Eventually one of them is going to blow up and he or she will blame you. If you want to have a long and successful career, stay away from people who seem bent on losing their money. That may seem like an odd thing to say, but there are self-destructive personalities out there. Some people hurt themselves with alcohol or drugs, some do it by gambling, and others do it by making irrational moves in the financial markets. Learn to say no to business that doesn't match your business strategy and/or your MPR standards.

CHAPTER FOUR

SELF-TALK AND PSYCHOLOGY

*Whether you think you can or
you think you can't . . . you are right.*

HENRY FORD

Think Yourself There

Your clients and prospects will perceive you just as you perceive yourself. If you feel you're an average producer, they are going to think you're average, too. However, if you refuse to get caught up in the negative self-talk of the average failure (in my book, being average *means* failure) and decide right now that you are a Top Gun producer, *that's* the image you will project. You are what you tell yourself you are. If you believe you're on the road to greatness, who is going to doubt you? People want to do business with people who *kick ass*. I don't know about you, but when I hire someone to work for me, I want that person to be the best. Everyone wants that. When was the last time you heard a woman brag about going to a second-rate hairstylist?

31

Have you ever heard anyone singing the praises of a doctor who treated him or her like one of a herd? Of course not! There isn't a person on earth who, given a choice, would take less than stellar service. Here it is in simple terms: See yourself as the best in the business and then work like a dog to make your vision real.

High Performance Thinking for Business, Sports, and Life, by Dr. Gayle Davis, PhD, is an excellent guide to the mental game of performance improvement. In the book she says:

> "The subconscious mind is just like a computer—it takes what you put in; it doesn't question; it takes input as fact and gives it back. If you tell yourself one thing enough times, or you hear something enough times, you create a habit or a belief. Since we have total control over what we think, what we choose to say to ourselves is one of most important choices. The content of our self-talk creates feeling, which leads to behavior. Negative self-talk will become negative behavior, positive self-talk will become positive behavior."

It is truly that simple.

As Davis points out in her book, there have been many studies to suggest that it takes 21 days of consistent behavior to either make or break a habit. That means you either have to exhibit the behavior you *want* to adopt for 21 days straight or not do the behavior you want to quit for 21 days straight. If you screw up, you have to start all over and go 21 days *in a row* of either adopting or abstaining from that specific behavior. This doesn't mean that you'd never go back to your old ways. What it does mean is that you'd have to *work* at it. After 21 days your natural tendency will be to continue the behavior you've either started or stopped. It would feel odd for you to go back to your old ways.

As an experiment, pick something simple you'd like to change about yourself and do something to create a new habit for 21 days. If you're going to try this, it's really important that you play by the rules. You've got to either do or not do whatever it is for the full 21 days. If you break for *any* reason, you must be honest about starting again. Maybe you want to get in shape. You could commit to walking on the treadmill for 20 minutes a day. Perhaps you'd like to become well read. You could commit to reading 10, 20, 30 pages of classic literature per day. As you succeed, you can wake up each day feeling more confident about other things in your life.

Look in the mirror and say to yourself, "I am a Top Producer. I am number one in my office." If you start acting like a top producer, communicating like a top producer, dressing like a top producer, and working like a top producer—in 21 days you will have developed the habits of a top producer. See if that doesn't come across to the people you deal with each day.

I tried it. I wanted pushups to be a daily habit, both the kind I do at home to improve my physical health and the kind I do at work to attract new business. I started by doing 10 pushups every night before bed and making 10 cold calls every day at work. I figured *something* had to improve . . . either my strength or my client list. I would have been happy with either. Before long I was doing 30, 40, 50 pushups every night and making 20, 30 new contacts every day at work. The confidence started building, both physically and mentally. The business started to come in. My clothes started to fit better. My confidence level rose, and authentic confidence has a smell all its own. People get a whiff and they want to get close to it.

See Yourself There

Another chapter in Dr. Davis' book is devoted to visualization. Any athlete will tell you that visualization techniques are a critical part of their training. Why? Because visualization enhances performance. It works. You know what they say, *if you can see it, you can be it.* As another exercise, think of something you desire. A new house, a new car, a new motorcycle, a fine piece of furniture, or an exclusive club membership. Close your eyes and see yourself enjoying that object of desire. Put yourself and your family in that house, in that car, sitting comfortably on that great piece of furniture. Picture yourself at the exclusive club in the wood-paneled library, talking to the other club members, sipping your favorite drink in a fine cut crystal glass. Really see yourself in the situation you desire or in the house of your dreams. Feel yourself behind the wheel of that incredible automobile. Drive by the house you want. Go test drive the car. Visualize yourself and your family in the home, using the yard, playing in the pool, sitting in the library reading a good book.

In baseball we were taught to visualize ourselves at bat. The next time you're at a game, watch the batter on deck, preparing to hit. Watch what he does. He will probably have his eyes closed. He's not praying (that happens earlier for most of us), he's "seeing" himself up at bat. He'll see the pitcher going into the windup and releasing the ball. He'll even see the seams of the ball as it comes toward the plate. He recognizes the pitch. He sees himself begin the swing and sees the bat make perfect contact with the ball. He pictures his follow-through. By the time he's really at bat, he's already been there in his mind, already rehearsed the perfect at-bat experience.

This is vitally important if you are to succeed and maintain your success because, as Davis states, "It is very difficult, if not impossible, to be successful at something that we really don't want to do or be." This sounds simple but is actually pretty deep. If you cannot see yourself being number one or being in the top 10 percent of the sales force, then any Top Gun techniques you get here or any other books you read on sales are not going to work. You will sabotage your own success if you don't believe you can attain it or deserve it. If you *do* have doubts about your success, it's important to look at the reason. Perhaps sales isn't really your bag. Maybe you see yourself succeeding at something else entirely. Maybe, for some reason, you don't think you deserve tremendous success. You'll often see people who become very successful for a short period and then they crash. They are one-hit wonders. They can't sustain the success. That's because they're uncomfortable with all the glory and subsequent pressure that comes along with stardom. The change is too much to handle. Some people really don't think they are deserving of such accolades. Let me tell you, if you do the work, you'll deserve its rewards.

The human mind is a curious, mysterious, and enormously powerful instrument. But it can be taught, and basically it will do what you tell it to do. If you don't believe you can perform at the top level, your mind will sabotage your efforts to do so. It's really only carrying out the picture you placed there. On the other hand, if you consistently tell your brain that you're going to the top and see yourself there, it will allow you to accomplish extraordinary feats. Again, your mind is simply doing as it has been told.

I'd like to share a story about two kids I grew up with. The first is Darryl. Darryl and I met a few times on and off the baseball field in California. This kid had more God-given talent for playing ball than virtually anyone I had ever seen. Even till this day, I haven't seen another ballplayer who could hit, run, and throw as naturally as Darryl. This kid was destined for stardom. Everyone who ever saw him felt the same way. It was no surprise when he was offered a professional baseball contract. He did become very famous. Guess where Darryl Strawberry is today? Prison. People can give you their reasons, explanations, and excuses for this ending. I think it's quite simple—Darryl could not handle his own success. Maybe, because his skills came *so* naturally, he didn't think he deserved the glory. Perhaps the responsibility of being a role model didn't appeal to him. It's also possible that the commitment required to be a member of a professional baseball team (daily practice, healthy diet, regular exercise, early to bed, staying out of trouble, publicity appearances, charity events, etc.) proved to be too much pressure.

Clearly, Darryl was uncomfortable with the changes in his life. To you and me the changes seem like good things. Even hard work seems well worth the rewards. But to him, the changes took him out of his area of comfort. Darryl was more at ease doing drugs with his old buddies from the neighborhood than being a successful professional baseball star. He sabotaged himself right out of a brilliant career. He probably could have been a hall of fame player. Even the consequence of prison was more palatable to Darryl than being a celebrity athlete. Can you imagine being more comfortable in *prison* than being a star? But that's exactly where the sum total of his decisions in life had led him.

The other kid I want to tell you about is Leon. For an athlete, even a baseball player, Leon was considered small. He was fairly short and very skinny. But Leon loved baseball so much he could think of little else. All things considered, he was a pretty good player, though nowhere near the caliber of player that Darryl was. The scouts told Leon he would never make it in the major leagues because he was too small. He was fast, but not fast enough, they said. He was strong, but not strong enough. Beyond his struggle on the baseball field, Leon didn't have an easy time of it at home, either. His father was a drug addict, and Leon lived all the nightmares associated with an abusive, drug-addicted parent every day.

God bless him. At age 16 he was told he'd never be able to achieve his only real dream and, instead of going home to comfort and solace, he went home to hell on earth. But Leon didn't give up. Nor did he dwell on what the scouts told him. The person he did listen to was his high school coach who told him to ignore the scouts and go after his dream. At the same time that he saw Darryl get drafted and collect a huge signing bonus, Leon drove himself to the middle of nowhere and hooked on to a combined team—a minor league team made up of a bunch of minor league players from numerous teams. This is the lowest minor league team you can join. He played for peanuts. But he was playing professional baseball! How great was that? What Leon lacked in natural talent, he more than made up for in heart. He gave baseball everything he had, and then some. He learned to switch hit. He worked out and bulked up. I don't know how he did it, but he became a faster runner, a better base stealer.

Want to know how this story turned out? Leon ended up playing in the major leagues for 11 seasons. He was well liked and well respected. He played in *several* championships and was voted onto the All-Star team. He retired from baseball at 39 years old, moved his family back to our old neighborhood where he lives and works today as a high school baseball coach. He's not on television every day, he isn't mobbed on the streets. In fact, he lives a pretty quiet life. But, to me, Leon is a superstar in every sense of the word.

I grew up with both of these men. Their backgrounds and neighborhoods were very similar. The difference between them lies in what they visualized for themselves. Leon saw himself as pro baseball player. He envisioned that life for himself and refused to change the picture. He would do whatever it took to achieve that goal, make any and all changes necessary. It didn't matter that a couple of strangers who didn't know him from Adam saw a different picture, even if they *were* professional scouts. Let them visualize their *own* lives. Leon believed in Leon. Period. As for Darryl, it's hard to believe he actually *wanted* to end up in prison, even if all his choices indicated otherwise. He was simply unwilling to leave his comfort zone, unwilling to change his ways. He didn't envision another kind of life for himself. He couldn't maintain the picture of success in his mind.

When your vision remains focused and you take action, your mind will subconsciously move you in the direction required to turn your pictures into reality. Visualization helps you align your actions with your desired results. You'll be ready to handle whatever roadblocks you come in contact with along the way, because what was once your dream has now become your expected and comfortable destiny. You belong in the picture you have in your mind. The picture in your mind is the comfort zone. Not getting there is uncomfortable.

I keep a saying on a wall in my office. It reads, "FAITH leads to BELIEF leads to ACTION leads to RESULTS." I keep it there not only for my benefit, but also for the benefit of everyone on the team. I can tell when they're worried, when business has been slow. It's part of my job, as team captain, to keep us all going through the difficult times. It's easy to be positive when things are going well. I tell my people the same thing I'm going to tell you now. There is absolutely no doubt in my mind, even in a time like this when the whole world seems to be out of control, that we're going to come out of it on the other side better off. There is always business to be had. Big business. Sometimes you have to be a little more creative in where you look for it.

I had a baseball coach who once handed everyone on the team a piece of paper and a pencil after a practice. He told us to write down everything we saw in the locker room. Thinking this was odd, but never to argue with the boss, we began writing. Lockers, benches, showers, towels, uniforms, clothes, watches, soap, shampoo, jock straps, players, coaches, bats, gloves, balls, face masks, we wrote it *all* down. When everyone was finished writing, he asked us if we were absolutely sure we didn't see anything else. After checking and rechecking our lists, we assured him that we had listed everything. Then the coach told us to stand up on the benches in the locker room. To our surprise, there were all kinds of bills spread out on top of the lockers.

Fives, tens, and twenties. A small fortune for a student! He said that if any one of us would have thought to look at the room from a new and different perspective by standing on top of the bench, we would have seen the money. He would have given that money to whomever had seen it first. If you don't like the view from where you're standing, stand someplace else. There is always another way to see any situation.

- *Faith.* Have faith in yourself and your capabilities. God gave us all strengths and unique talents. If you haven't found yours yet, keep searching. They are there. Maybe you just need to look from a different angle.

- *Belief.* Your faith will give you something to believe in. If you believe you can swim across the English Channel, then diving in the water isn't a big deal, is it? If you believe you can build a $5 million book, picking up the phone is just the first step, right?

- *Action.* When you believe wholeheartedly that you are capable of accomplishing something and have sustained a vision of that accomplishment, taking action is what will make it happen for you. Remember that vision without action is a daydream, and action without vision is a nightmare. You need both to achieve success.

- *Results.* You get results when you consistently act upon your vision. It's self-fulfilling. If you do the work, the results take care of themselves. Discover your niche, learn more than anyone else knows about that niche, make your cold calls, visit prospective clients, and take great care of the ones you already have. Do this every day. You won't have any other *choice* but to achieve results.

Resist Negative Talk

Negative talk runs rampant in our business. I'll tell you why. It's because there is an incredible amount of pressure. Not only is there pressure to make our numbers, but when people and/or corporations turn their money over to us to handle, a mistake on our part could have devastating effects to the client and to us. It's a huge responsibility, and it's natural to want to shoulder some of it. In order to do that, you can't go around saying everything's great. If you work for the best firm, for the most honorable boss, have the most efficient secretary, and are doing business in a thriving market, . . . who is left to blame if things go awry? Nobody but you.

If you have internal problems with a team member, discuss them one on one. The same thing applies if you have a problem with your boss. Make an appointment and discuss it honestly and *privately.* Never bad-mouth a member of your firm. Most of us spend more awake time with the people we work with than with our own families these days. Staying loyal strengthens the team. It makes you a united force. As far as blaming the market goes . . . sure, these are unusual times. But they are unusual for *everyone* in the business. Why don't you let the *rest* of the financial world complain about the market? In the meantime, you go out and take away their business.

While we're on the subject of negativity, let's have some straight talk about money. In some circles, a person's drive to make a grand living is perceived as something less than noble. I think that's a bunch of crap. Money is important. Having money is really important. Not having money sucks. Not because you can't join the jet set, but because stuff happens. People in your family—your kids for example—might need help that is expensive. Your parents' health might not be the best and you need to pay for something for them. People who don't think that money is important either have a lot of it, have no responsibilities, or are jealous. Jealous people envy your ability to provide the best for your family without questioning the cost. They'll also be the first people in line to borrow money from you when they need it.

CHAPTER FIVE

THE TOP GUN MODEL RULES OF ENGAGEMENT

*The dictionary is the only place
where success comes before work.*

VINCE LOMBARDI

Never Have More Than 50 Client Relationships

There's more than one in every office. You know, the guy whose phone rings off the hook all day. He has 4,000 clients who run him ragged. He's always in the "catch-up" mode. He's frantic, he's harried and, quite frankly, he's a mess. Someone is upset with him at all times, either for a mistake he's made or for lack of attention. To add insult to injury, the poor schmo is an average performer . . . at *best*.

You would think that with all this activity he'd be doing well over a million dollars in business. But he's not. In fact, he has rarely achieved $500,000 in his career. His problem is very simple. He has too many clients and way too many of the *wrong type* of clients. Trust me, I know this guy well. His type is everywhere. In fact, a long time ago I was one of them.

Here's the logic I work by today. If 20 percent of your clients provide 80 percent of your revenue, then the other 80 percent of your clients are paying only 20 percent of your revenue. Right? That's a lot of effort for 20 percent, don't you think? Why not simply get rid of the 80 percent of your clients who only pay 20 percent of your revenue? You could then take on a few more of those high margin clients who are currently paying the majority of your income. You wouldn't have to work so hard, for so little. You'll make *more* money. You'd have more time to spend on the things that *add* to your life. Free up time to work on landing other high margin clients and spend some time with your family.

This is really the heart and soul of Top Gun, and it's a *big* change. I'm suggesting you *drop 80 percent of your book* right away! I have a lot of nerve, don't I? Don't worry, you're going to thank me . . . and sooner than you think. Here's how you do it. Go through your records for the last few years and take a good hard look at your numbers. Rank all your clients by revenue for each year. Any client who appears in the top 20 percent for all three years, mark with an A+. Any client who appears in the top 20 percent for two years, mark with an A. Finally, any client who appears in the top 20 percent for one year, give an A-. Now you have a list of your A clients. The next step is to remove from that list those clients who are no longer doing business with you, those clients who have died, and those clients who are rapidly decreasing their business. From the group you have left, remove those clients who are problems, the people with whom you really don't enjoy working. Everyone who is left on the list is your new client base. The rest must go. It's that simple. Or, it will be after you pass these clients on to a junior broker. Make a deal with him or her or a registered assistant to pay for their handling of this business. Now, cross those clients off your list of things to worry about. You don't ever have to talk to them again. You are moving on.

I suggest you offer these clients to a junior broker or a registered assistant and share the revenue for six months to a year. This is a reasonable time frame for them to see the benefit of taking them on, and it pays you for any transition issues. Now you can cross this group of clients off your list and never think about their problems again. You never have to talk to them again. They don't take up any more of your brain space. This allows your brain to be free to accept new clients, better clients, ones that will fit the profile you want going forward. It also frees up your time to go after them.

That may sound cold and callous, but the truth is, you can't provide those clients who pay you top dollar with your highest level of thinking and best possible service if you're too busy with clients who aren't maximizing your talent. Again, I must go on record saying that *everyone* has a right to invest their money. Everyone is entitled to money management. But, this isn't a charity. Everyone isn't entitled to *your* time. You have made an investment in your business, your firm has made an investment in you, and this is a for-profit business you and I are engaged in. A good client wants you to make money so that you'll be there to serve him or her another day. As a Top Gun producer (or someone well on the way to becoming one), you deserve Top Gun clients. Let people with lesser ambitions tend to the others. If you are a single practitioner, you don't need more than 50 great clients. If you're a team, perhaps you need 150 to 175 clients to get over the 5 million dollar mark.

Bring a Higher Level of Thinking to Your Clients

After you've eliminated 80 percent of your clients, you'll probably feel a little exposed. Maybe you'll wonder what the *hell* you've done. This is just mental bullshit, your mind being uneasy about dealing with change. The truth is, you were probably in danger of losing one of your top 20 percenters if you *didn't* lighten your load. You were exposed anyway, you just didn't know it.

So, now you can go on the offensive. Believe me, this feels a lot better than being on the defensive. First thing you need to do is meet face to face with your new client base. Tell them this exactly: "I just voluntarily turned over 80 percent of my clients to other brokers. The reason I did this was because I had become too busy to provide my most *important* clients with the kind of service and higher thinking that they deserve. *You* are one of my most valued clients, and from now on I'm going to devote more of my time to your financial affairs." Then watch what happens.

You're Never Too Big to Go Prospecting

Probably the best reason to continue to prospect, even after you've become a Top Gun, is that prospecting keeps you sharp. It makes you aware of competitive dangers. You hear what's happening with the business in your market. People will tell you what financial options interest them and why. This is valuable information to you. You'll be able to keep abreast of competitive threats which will allow you to make the changes necessary to keep your clients informed and happy. Besides that, your once-in-a-lifetime client is only a prospect away.

Prospecting also helps to keep you confident. With confidence comes the power to say no to clients who are unreasonable in their requests. You can run your business the way *you* think is right and send those who disagree to other brokers. If you have the activity of many prospects, saying no to one or two is easy. If you don't prospect, every prospect feels so important to your future business, you feel you can't turn them away. It gives you the power to say no to clients who are asking you to be unreasonable. Prospecting keeps you young in this business. The financial world changes too quickly to remain stagnant.

Still, prospecting can seem like a brutal task. Sometimes it seems like you're not getting anywhere, that you'll never get a worthy client again. Don't let that deter you. Look at it this way. Picture a human-made dam, holding back a small lake. Every call you make is a bucket of water you are putting into the lake, adding pressure to the dam. You keep adding a bucket, adding a bucket, and soon, the dam begins to leak. The dam begins to crack, and soon you see a major break. The calls start coming back, the flow of prospects picks up, the meetings start rolling in, and you're closing business. This is how it happens. It won't happen if you don't keep adding the buckets of water to the lake.

That life-changing client is out there. I've been through every major financial crisis on Wall Street since 1980. I've built and rebuilt five books of business. Now I look at my book as a constantly changing thing—something that is never static—it is constantly being rebuilt to upgrade its quality of clientele and access new market opportunities for my team.

Sell to the Strengths of the Firm

Every firm has a distinct set of strengths and weaknesses. Your job as a salesperson, as well as being a valuable asset to your firm, is to know what they are. Find out from the president of the firm or head of sales for the company the SWOT matrix. SWOT stands for Strengths, Weaknesses, Opportunities, and Threats. Compiling this report is an exercise senior management goes through regularly. Ask the other top salespeople what is selling, what the latest trends are. Be leery of anyone who encourages you to "push" a certain product. We serve our clients' needs, we don't push products on them. Go to the guys in the trenches for information. They'll tell you what's up. They're the ones who know what's working and what isn't.

Every firm has a few very significant strengths. This is where you start drilling. Learn why the firm is strong in these areas. Find out who runs them and make it a point to meet and become friendly with him and her. Who are the firms' best customers in these areas. Is the market still growing? Who are the firms' biggest competitors? Why do we beat them (or why don't we)? You need to know the story, so you can *tell* the story. Remember, in the business of sales, it's the story that sells. If you don't know the stories, you can't sell. Always sell to the strength of your firm. You're not a missionary—you're a salesperson.

Salespeople are paid on commission (or fees in our case). In order to make as much as possible, you've got to sell as much as possible. Leave the big experiments to a salaried employee.

Shorter Sales Cycles = Higher Sales (90 Days, Tops)

Later in the book I tell you about a case in which we applied our "surrounding the trade" strategy to win a big piece of seven-figure business. From the time we first met the client to the day the wire hit, the account was about five weeks. Shorter sales cycles = more business. It goes back to the original screening process. Good screening will put you in front of people who are liquid and can make a decision on the spot. At the very least, they'll be able to commit to a change within the next 30 to 45 days. When you get in front of these kinds of people, you should be able to close the deal on the spot, the next day, or within a few weeks, tops. Every day that goes by past 30, your chances of closing diminish.

The mistake most of us make is in believing that we continue to build a relationship with a prospect over a year or two of discussion. If you believe this, you're fooling yourself. We build relationships with clients, not prospects. I can't tell you how many brokers I know who spend years chasing prospects. None of them do over $1 million in business. Average brokers live on hope. Not you. If you have been "courting" anyone for more than a year who has yet to give you their business, pick up the phone. It's time to fill or kill.

I like to tell prospects that I have two lists, one in black and one in red. The black list contains the names of clients. These people get the first call, the best advice, the best service, the best deals, the best of everything from me. They are on the "A" list. The other list contains the names of prospective clients. They talk about becoming clients, but they always have a reason for delaying. I suggest you offer them a last chance invitation to join the "A" list, and indicate that you would be honored if they would accept. You can even tell them that it's okay to say no, but you'd just like to know because you don't want to continue to bother them. This is a nice guy fill or kill. Either answer is fine with you. If they decline your invitation to become a client and join the "A" list, by forcing the issue, you've just done yourself a favor. This person would have danced with you forever, but never would have gone home with you. Feel good about the ones who decline. They've just stopped wasting your time.

One on One, One by One

Meet with your top prospects face to face. Seminars, mailers, and letters of introduction are for losers. These things waste time and money, and more importantly, they don't work. Pick up the phone, talk to someone. Go out and meet them. State your case. Give them three or four valid reasons to do business with you. Differentiate yourself from others in the first meeting. Then leave.

Diversify into Two or Three Noncorrelated Business Lines

Being a one-trick pony is okay if you happen to be in the right business line. The problem is that I have seen too many times when this business line was eliminated or scaled back by the firm. This can dislocate you and make you and your family vulnerable. You become vulnerable to shifts in the business or your particular firm's strategy.

Having a few noncorrelated lines of business is important. When the equity markets are in a raging bull, that's good for an equity person, but what happens when the bear comes to town? Your income can get cut in half, even if it is fee-only business. When markets get cut in half, so do your assets under management, and the fees go down with it.

Alternatively, you may have a partner that specializes in bonds. By combining your businesses, he and you will ride out the tough markets for your respective business areas by sharing fees. There will be periods where you produce a ton in the equity markets, which you share with him. Then there will be periods when he is doing big business in bonds while your equity business has been cut in half.

If you build your book to have steady fee business in two or three noncorrelated areas, then you will be able to ride out the market volatility and the cycles that each are certain to be subject to.

Create Discretionary or Managed Accounts for 90 Percent of Your Business

There is no way you can hit huge numbers if you have to make a phone call every time you have to do a piece of business. It just won't happen. You need to structure your business such that you are making the decisions on the majority of the accounts, whether that be a quarterly asset allocation change, or making buy and sell decisions for a structure method of doing business within the guidelines of the client and the firm.

Eliminate Negative People in Your Life

There are some moments in your life that make impressions that last forever. I once had a great friend named Marty. I realized he was a great friend when he kicked me out of his car on the 405 Freeway in Los Angeles one night at 11:00 PM. The truth be told, I had been complaining nonstop for the entire evening. I was just a downer. There's no other way to describe it. Finally, he could take it no longer and told me so. He simply explained he had made a decision for his own well-being not to be around negative people any more. It would have been one thing if I had an authentic problem. What he couldn't stand was my ranting and raving about everything. He asked if there was something seriously wrong. When I told him there wasn't, he said life was too short to listen to people's crap. He was right. A good friend will tell you stuff like that, pointing out your stupidity and weaknesses in an effort to make you a better person.

Your clients don't want to call a person who is a downer. Who does? Your manager doesn't want someone in the office who complains all the time, whines about stuff, and is generally a pain in the ass. Would you? Your assistant, your partners—they don't want someone who is Mr. Negative around them all day every day. These people can find something else to do, someone else to do it with. You can be serious and work hard and care about what you're doing without being negative.

Your attitude is your choice. It is only controlled by your clients, others in the office, your wife, your neighbor, the market, or your enemies *if you let them.*

Embrace Change

Our business and the world is always changing. If you can't roll with the changes and look at them from an angle that is positive—make them work for you—then you're going to have a hard time getting through life.

Keep Your Reward Close to You Every Day

Have a reward in mind that is tied to a goal that is business oriented. Whether that goal is reaching a certain title, or a certain production threshold, have a reward in mind that you will give yourself when it happens. Keep it close to you by putting a picture of it on your desk or somewhere that you can see it every day, reminding you of something really good that is going to happen if you just keep at it.

Always Take Closing Paperwork with You, Even to the First Meeting

Don't ever assume that you can't do business on the first call. You can. I have done so many, many times. Be prepared.

Don't Ever Compromise Your Business Ethics, Philosophies, or Rules

The fastest way to get into trouble is to compromise the foundations of your business ethics or philosophies. A career is very long. How much money can you possibly make by compromising those things that are worth your reputation and your career?

Decide *Not* to be Average

Average. America is not about being average. America is about winners. Who aspires to be average? Who wants to do business with an average person? Who goes to an average doctor or uses an average lawyer? Come on!

Protect Your Time, Your Reputation, and Your Ideas . . . *Fiercely*

We don't have a lot that is proprietary in our business, but your ideas are, and your best assets are your time, talent, and reputation. If anyone messes with those things, they are striking at the heart of what you bring to the game every day, and you need to call them on it and protect yourself.

Listen to the Music, Hear What People *Aren't Saying*

Read between the lines. People will often dance around a subject but give you clues to their real concerns. Sometimes a client can call up and seem angry, but what he's really telling you is that he is scared and wants you to reassure him. If you react incorrectly, you can lose the client. Listen to the *music* in his words, not just the words.

Top 10 Percent Office Production, Bottom 20 Percent Office Expenses

If you can achieve this consistently, the firm will always want you in your seat. The firm wants high productivity. They want profitable people in their seats. If you're in the top 10 percent of the producers and have a cost structure in the bottom 20 percent of all the firm's brokers, you will always be wanted.

Rehearse—Then Rehearse Again

Like Tiger Woods, rehearsal is the price you pay for greatness. You can't make it look easy if you don't rehearse.

CHAPTER SIX

FIRST STEPS

Nosce Te Ipsum

LATIN, MEANING "KNOW THYSELF"

The Top Gun Producer Process

1. Assess yourself

2. Assess your business and clients

3. Assess your firm's "weapons"

4. Choose your weapons

5. Focus, concentrate, and plan

6. Practice and rehearse

7. Execute and perform

8. Assess the results

9. Make adjustments

10. Go back to number 6

Structuring Your Business

Dr. Gayle Davis in *High Performance Thinking for Business, Sports, and Life* reminds us that planning is like the story of Alice in Wonderland when she is approaching the fork in the road and sought directions from the Cheshire Cat. Upon approaching the cat, Alice asked whether she should go left or go right. Before he would answer, he wanted to know where it was she wanted to go. Alice replied that she had no idea where it was she wanted to go. The cat informed her that it really didn't matter then if she went to the right or the left. In other words, you need to have an idea of where you want to go with your business.

There are three major things you have to deal with in structuring your business for the future:

1. What products and services are you going to represent and to whom?

2. What is the best way for you to deliver these services and products to your clients—as part of a team or as a lone wolf?

3. What systems, processes, people, and other resources do you need in order to effectively and efficiently do the job?

In going through the following process, you will come up with the right answers to these questions for yourself. At the end of the exercise, you should have a good idea of the products and services you want to utilize in your business—and you will have chosen them because they feel right for you. You will know whether or not a team approach to delivering these things to your clients is the right approach for you and for them. You will also know what resources you'll need in order to get the job done efficiently and effectively.

The process of transforming your business starts by asking and answering some questions.

Assess Yourself and Give Your Business Some Direction

- What am I passionate about in the workplace—what do I love to do?

- Is there a market for what I love to do?

- What do I hate to do?

- What am I good at?

- What are my weaknesses?

- Can I outsource my areas of weakness?

The answers to these questions will help direct you to the type of business you focus on and to the type you should delegate. The beauty of financial sales is that if we are weak in an area, or don't like it, most of the time we can choose not to do it. We can either delegate it or can choose not to do it at all. For example—I dislike the 401(k) plan business for a variety of reasons. But I also know that 401(k) plans can be a steady source of revenue. I have two options: 1) I can not do 401(k) plans; 2) I can, if I come across a great opportunity in this area, turn it over to a specialist or another professional who enjoys working 401(k) plans, let that person excel, and share the revenue stream. Another example is fixed income. I like fixed income, but I'm just not as good at it as others. It doesn't come naturally to me, and I don't have the time or the desire to get the experience I'd need to *be* good at it. But there are people all around me who know the fixed income world cold. They dream about bonds in their sleep! Why should I risk a major client relationship by making a mistake or giving less than my best? Doesn't it make sense to outsource that part of the business to someone who will serve my client the way he and she deserves? The other broker and I share the revenue, and the client receives the best advice possible. It's a win/win/win situation!

Now, you may find some advisors and brokers who aren't too keen on sharing client revenues. I think that attitude is archaic. I share business regularly and, in exchange, other professionals share their business with me. We have to keep reminding ourselves that we're in the *service* business. We sell a service. It's in the clients' best interests to give them the finest service their money can buy.

Assess Your Business and Clients

One of the biggest differences between the average producer and a Top Gun producer is the quality of their clients. You rarely catch a Top Gun complaining about a client. We don't work with people we don't like. We don't spend our energy catering to nut-cases. There is a mutual exchange of respect between client and broker. Our clients trust us unequivocally, and as a result, it is our pleasure to serve them well. This is why the scaling down of your book is so important. It frees you up to be a better stockbroker to the people who pay you top dollar. When assessing your business, ask yourself the following questions. Try to make your answers as specific as possible. The clearer you can focus on the type of business you'd like to run, the better off you'll be.

- With what type of people do I want to do business?

- With what type of company do I enjoying working?

- What are the reasons for these choices?

- How many of my chosen type of clients will I need in order to do $5 million or $10 million in production?

- How much do I want to be paid, per client relationship, to take on a new client or relationship?

Questions surrounding the types of clients you want to work with are probably the most important questions you need to answer. Once you come to terms with the fact that you *aren't* going to take any and every client who comes your way, you can concentrate on going after the business that *you* desire. You have too much to accomplish to be weighed down with clients that don't add to the quality of your life and the profitability of your business. In the same respect, when people hire someone to handle their money, they deserve to have someone who really cares about their business. It's unfair to take on their business and not give it your all.

Assess Your Firm's "Weapons"

At this point in the process, you should be fairly clear on both the type of business you want to do and the type of people you want to do it with. Just saying you want to work with rich clients doesn't cut it. We *all* want to work with rich clients. What do you want to do for *them?* What can you offer your clients that's special or different? It's time to look to your firm to see how their tools, products, and services can support your agenda and how your special skills can support your firm.

- What products and services does the firm have that are aligned with who I am?

- What are the competitive strengths of the firm?

- What are the firm's consistent sources of highly profitable revenues, and can I drive business to those sources?

- What is my process—internally and externally?

Your personal Top Gun business model can be designed once you've got a firm grasp on which products and services you want to utilize in conjunction with the strengths of your firm and the current trends in the local and national market. The Boston Matrix, developed by the Boston Consulting Group, is a tool designed to analyze all of this information. Use the framework of their model to categorize the service and product offerings of your firm. You know which products and services you want to represent to the market, but the Boston Matrix will help you to know where each of these products and services lie in the mix as we go forward. This is important because it is imperative for long-term survival on the street to know where the risks lie in your business plan.

For example, not many years ago there were thousands and thousands of brokers all over the country doing nothing but municipal bond business. One hundred percent of their business was dependent upon the trading of municipal bonds. This business was dependent upon the firm maintaining a robust inventory of municipal bonds for sale. There was virtually no thought that the firm may get out of the municipal bond business. You simply had to be in it. Then the business consolidated, and many firms stopped doing business in the municipal bond market altogether. Surprise! These folks were displaced because they didn't know anything else. Not a good place to be. This is why we talk about diversifying your business into at least two lines of business, and ideally three. We've also talked about not being all things to all people, and that's still true. With four or five business lines, you're probably facing diminishing returns. Three lines of business is optimal even in a large team. Grow what you do well before expanding your lines of business.

The Boston Matrix

You can use the Boston Matrix to segment the products and services in your business to help you assess your current business and decide which products and services you want to add or delete from your current model.

FIGURE 6.1   Boston Matrix

	High **MARKET SHARE** Low	
High M A R K E T G R O W T H **Low**	**STARS** High market share in high growth markets. Require cash for growth but have strong competitive position and should be invested in.	**QUESTION MARKS** Require a lot of capital for growth, but have not yet gained enough market share to be a highly profitable enterprise. Can become a DOG or a STAR. An unknown.
	CASH COWS High market share in low growth markets. They do not require much capital to maintain their position and their cash can be used for STARS.	**DOGS** Cash loser or cash trap. Weak or no profits. Should be turned around quickly or eliminated. Not candidates for serious investment dollars or resource allocation.

Let's take a look at this matrix (Figure 6.1). The Stars are High Margin, High Growth businesses. Cash Cows are high margin businesses for which the demand in the market is not growing rapidly, but it is still a good stable solid business. Cash Cows provide you with the capital to invest in Stars. To be located in these sectors of the matrix, your firm needs to have a competitive offering in this area and be committed to maintaining or increasing its market share, otherwise it can't fit here for you. If your firm isn't competitive in this area and isn't committed to this business for the long term, then why should you add it to your portfolio of client offerings?

You'll be outgunned by the competition, and the execution of your business plan will fall apart no matter how good you

FIGURE 6.2   Adapted Boston Matrix

	High MARKET SHARE Low	
High M A R K E T G R O W T H **Low**	**STARS** Insurance Products Structured Products Hedging transactions Derivative Based Lending Hedge Funds Private Equity Funds Swaps	**QUESTION MARKS** Stock Option Plans Stock Purchase Plans 529 Plans Commercial Lending
	CASH COWS Consulting Equity/Fixed Income Managed Accounts Cash Management Currency Exchange 10b-18 Buybacks Mutual Funds	**DOGS** Trading Accounts Lock Box 401(k) Plans

are, and you won't be successful—through no fault of your own. The problem could lie in the pricing, the support, or the operating systems. It's a direct result of a business line that your firm is not committed to maintaining or growing. Although you can't control that, you need to be able to recognize it.

Most firms are committed to having a decent offering in the Managed Account business, or wrap fee asset management. Third Party Managers are selected and through some process you deliver the right ones to your clients based upon the answers to the questionnaire. This is basic "bread and butter" business, nothing fancy. If your firm has competitive fees, you can build a decent business here. It may be debatable as to whether this is a Cash Cow business or a Star business. With the transfer of wealth we see coming from the folks in their 70s, 80s and 90s to people in their 40s, 50s and 60s, it could be a high growth business and qualify for Star status. Demand for investment services, and more important, good solid investment advice, should go up significantly over the next 20 years. Certainly because a whole new generation of young, intelligent people have experienced serious losses in the market with the bursting of the dot-com bubble, even these people now understand that getting good outside advice is necessary when managing large sums of money. So, even though fees in this area have come down somewhat, they are still good, profitable businesses—and there is a large market. One analyst estimates that there will be at least $80 billion annually rolling into IRA accounts from the boomers from 2005 to 2015.

This business meets the MPR test as well. (Check out Chapter 3.) The margin is there, the probability of people wanting and needing the service is there, and the risk is low. Once in place, it doesn't take much of your time to monitor the manager. Fortunately, you aren't responsible for the daily selection of stocks or bonds, which is tremendously time consuming . . . and therefore would lower your margin. You'd be using a professional outside money manager. This outside manager matches your clients' risk tolerance and needs. Allocating money with this manager will not throw portfolios off balance. The risk is low—a solid MPR business.

This is the selection ritual you need to go through with every product and service in your firm's arsenal of offerings to select the weapons for your Top Gun Model. It's an exercise every advisor should do over and over again throughout a career. It will also force you to be aware of shifts that may be occurring in your firm's resource allocation of which others may not be aware. My experience is that firms don't tell you where they are moving resources—you have to figure it out yourself. It's tremendously frustrating, but it is what it is.

You have to look around and see where the firm is making most of its money. If you see that the firm is making a ton of money doing equity derivative transactions, perhaps you should find out more about those and see if you can't drive business to that desk! If you see that you used to have 250 people on a municipal bond trading desk in New York, and now there are 15 people there, perhaps you should ask why, and make the appropriate adjustments to your own business. Whatever business lines you choose to offer, you should build a solid Cash Cow business first. This will allow you to expand into other areas that are Stars or potential Stars. Treat your business just like the CEO of a holding company who is responsible for managing a portfolio of companies.

Develop your own outline or process for your different types of business. Whatever businesses you decide to operate in, there is already an outline in place somewhere in your firm for each. Cash management. Asset management. Investment consulting. Derivatives. Foreign currency. Fixed income. Swaps. Private placements. Hedge funds. Restricted stock. Get to know the processes you need to know. Put your systems in place. Part of the value you can deliver to your new clients will be to put their financial affairs into the context of a proven plan. One of the gifts you can give yourself is a process you follow internally for your business. It makes your life easier, but more importantly, it makes it easier for your clients and your support staff to understand what you're doing.

Take it a step further. Make sure you have a method of delivering results that are measurable. Tell your clients how you measure results in the context of the business you're doing for them. Get them to sign off on that process of measurement up front, and deliver. Everyone in the equation, including you, will know how things are going. You won't be surprised if your client leaves you or is unhappy should the results be poor. In fact, if *you* are the one who mentions the poor results first, rather than wait until your client finds out for himself or herself, this client is more likely to stay with you through a temporary setback—because he or she knows you're honest *and* on top of your business!

Focus Your Business

Narrow your focus. One challenge with financial salespeople is really focusing on what they do well . . . and sticking to that. Too many of us try to be trading experts, a retirement planning expert, an options trader, a cash management expert, a venture capitalist, an investment banker, and a research analyst all by ourselves. We spread ourselves too thin, and we risk not doing any one thing consistently well.

Better to learn where the firm excels. Know the areas in which the firm consistently wins business. Is it in the $5 million account and below? Or is it in the $50 million dollar account and above? Know the competitive advantages, products, services of the firm, even if they are just perceived advantages. Once you have that knowledge, you can compete more successfully and you can decide if what you're doing is in line with where the firm is going.

Learn to say no to the business that doesn't fit MPR or your selections from the matrix. It will be tremendously freeing for you—and I assure you it will increase your production and productivity. You'll be doing what you like, with clients you like, and you will not only make more money, you'll be happier. Doesn't that sound like a better life than you have now, scrambling from one fire to the other, balls dropping everywhere, never able to keep up?

Focus, Concentrate, and Plan

With respect to taking on new clients, you need to set the minimums for your type of business that work for you. In the beginning, I used to tell the rookies, if you live in an apartment that charges you $1,250 a month, you can take any account that is $15,000 or more ($12 \times 1,250$). Once you've got a good number of those, maybe you'll be able to think about buying a house. If you're thinking about buying a $300,000 house, you cannot take any accounts less than $300,000. Once you own that house, you need to look at what kind of house you'd like to live in next. If the next house is a $700,000 house, you have to get accounts at that minimum or higher, and so on. Even if you're doing $2 million a year in gross commissions and fees, you can decide to bring your minimums to $5 million or $10 million.

But don't fool yourself. Whether you're doing $400,000 or $4 million annually, the production you deliver is dependent upon the decisions you make, who you work with, what products and services you offer, and to how many clients you offer them. These are the variables that will ultimately determine your long-term rate of production, not whether the market is going up or down or if rates are going up or down. Those factors have only short-term influences on your production.

Another myth of the financial sales business is that in order to do millions of dollars in production, you need to have a ton of assets under management. This is simply not true in all cases. Relationships are more important than assets. If you have relationships with the top 50 CFOs in the nation, and you end up swapping all their debt from fixed to floating one year, you may do $25 million in sales in the swaps, yet you hold no assets. Assets are only important if all your business lines involve charging a fee based upon assets held at your firm. What if you are a consultant who monitors the performance of other managers? What if those assets are held away, but you still make 15 basis points off those assets in order to monitor and provide reporting and analysis services? You have no assets directly under management, but you may gross $3 million or $4 million in production annually!

One way or another, you'll either make the decision to remain where you are or move your business to the next level. Whether you make that decision consciously or unconsciously—make no mistake about it—the decision will be made. Many people don't want to take a hard look at their business, be honest about it, and accept responsibility for where they are. After all, it's easier to blame the firm, blame your manager, blame your wife and kids, or something else. That's why so many people are average—because it's easy.

Many of you have the house you've always wanted. You have the car, the toys, the trips, whatever. You may be, as I was, dealing with clients you don't really enjoy working for, struggling to get to $500,000 a year in business, or maybe you've got a $2 million book. Either way, at some point you come to a crossroads and ask, "Now what?" You can look in the mirror and make the decision to go for the Top Gun ranks of our business. To be somebody that does $5 million to $10 million or more, or stay exactly where you are. It's entirely up to you.

What you have to do next, what you must do next, if you want to be one of the elite producers in our business, is the hard part. As I said earlier, most people can't do it, and I believe it is the primary reason why they remain average. You need to get rid of 80 percent of your book. You've got to clean house—get rid of the time wasters, the low margin, high effort clients who keep you from making the big numbers. It may sound radical, but it works. *Your book is the reason you're average!*

Constraints on Your Business Productivity

Time

There are only so many hours in each day and only so many phone calls you can make. If you construct your relationships such that you have to make a phone call every time a piece of business is going to get done, every time a trade has to be made, every time a bond or stock is swapped, you will fail. You simply cannot compete with someone who has constructed a streamlined business that does $2 million annually in fees without ever making a phone call.

Relationships

You can only talk to so many people per day. Are you talking to people with the power to act and make major financial decisions for their corporations or personal portfolios? Or are you just talking to someone who will listen? I call these nice, comfortable calls that produce no revenue, "Happy Calls." They leave you feeling all warm and fuzzy, but you haven't done any business.

Firm Capabilities

If you're working for a firm with limited reach in areas that are important to you in the matrix, then you're in trouble. Be sure you're in the right place for the future of your personal business and the business in general. That may mean you simply have to do more investigating at your current firm, or it may mean moving to another firm. It may mean being out on your own as an independent or quasi-independent. Only you can determine the right answers in this area.

Support Systems

Does your firm provide you with the appropriate information systems and execution capabilities for your business? Does your business require a number of support people in the back office, and does the firm have them in place? Does your business require that you have two, three, or four assistants in order to handle administrative issues? If so, will the firm provide them for you? Are you willing to pay for them? (Any business model that is producing less than $2 million per year that requires three or four assistants may be a low margin model to begin with and should be examined closely.)

Factors That Determine or Constrain Your Production

The Firm That Works for You

There are really two mindsets among the executives who run Wall Street firms today. One is the mindset that believes that you work for the firm and any clients you handle are ultimately the firm's clients, and *you* should be nothing but grateful to have a job there. Your boss would like nothing better than to see you appear at his door each morning to thank him for mercifully allowing you to work for the firm another day. Does that sound familiar? Of course, there *is* another mindset out there. In this one, upper management understands that you've worked damned hard to cultivate your client relationships and can take them anywhere you want to go. But, just as your clients have chosen to work with you, *you* have chosen to work with your firm. It's a mutually advantageous working arrangement. I have worked with both of these Wall Street mindsets. Under which do you think I became a Top Gun?

Capabilities of the Firm

With respect to constraints, the firm's capabilities determine what products and services you can offer and in what type of situations you can effectively and successfully execute.

If you have a firm that has a thin balance sheet, how are you going to execute a large derivative-based lending transaction? You're not. If you want to compete with the big boys in fixed income, and your firm buys its bonds from one of the big houses, how are you going to compete with them should they decide to target your customer and essentially cut you out? You're not. If you have a need for Bloomberg to execute fixed-income trades, monitor foreign currency exchange rates, see current swap rates, or use sophisticated analytics, and you're with a firm that won't give you access to Bloomberg, how are you going to do business? How are you going to compete? It's like taking a rabbit gun out into a battlefield of tanks. You're going to lose every time.

The Clients You Work For

When your clients decide to do something, do they give you a 10,000-share order? Does their account generate $2,500 annually in fees or does it generate $25,000 annually in fees? The time you spend is virtually the same in describing the transaction, the reallocation, the product or the service to each client! How do you want to spend your time and with whom? It is that simple.

The Products and Services You Offer

Are the services and products you offer "me too" kinds of things that clients can get from a 23-year-old kid wearing a $100 suit, sitting behind a Formica counter at a discount brokerage on Main Street? Do the things you talk to people about run the risk of becoming commoditized in the financial services market? Or do you provide a higher level of thinking to your clients? Better yet, do your clients require a higher level of thinking? If so, you move into the realm of higher margin products and services because you are adding value far beyond the kid at the counter.

The Number of Clients You Have

There is a direct correlation between the number of clients you have and your ability to provide higher levels of thinking and service. By adding real value you can drive margins for yourself and satisfaction to your clients. Simply put, you shouldn't have more than 50 client relationships per registered member of your team, including your assistant. If your assistant is registered, then your number is 100. If you share him and her with another broker, then you cut 50 in half and your number is 75. This is the formula. It's that simple. If you can't get your head around that, then put this book down and read something else because I cannot help you.

If Broker A has 50 client relationships that provide $250,000 each per year in fees, Broker A is doing $12.5 million per year in gross. That broker doesn't need ten assistants and junior brokers to do it. He has one very good, well-compensated, professional assistant and perhaps a junior or associate broker. Broker A is high margin to the firm. And here is where there's a disconnect on Wall Street. He gets paid at the same rate as Broker B, who requires five assistants and has 2,000 clients. Broker A is imminently more profitable than Broker B, isn't he? Broker A has exposure (risk) to only 50 clients—so he probably puts the firm at less risk, does he not? The firm should give Broker A a higher payout than they do Broker B. Broker B does the same amount of business but requires five assistants. At the very least, the firm should give Broker A more in deferred compensation and more expense money to take care of his high margin clients than they give Broker B with 2,000 clients and five assistants.

Think of the cost of sending monthly statements to 2,000 clients, confirms to 2,000 clients, as well as paying the salaries, healthcare, retirement benefits, parking, phone calls, and rent for five assistants instead of one! The broker with 2,000 clients sucks down a ton of human and financial resources of the firm. He also puts the firm at greater exposure. There are back office people who have to process all the statements, confirms, and reports. In addition, management and compliance must monitor 2,000 accounts for Broker B. Which broker do you think the firm should want? If the firm is cutting back personnel and has to make a decision as to who will stay and who will go, which one do you think they should keep? Which do you think they *will* keep?

The Minimum Requirements You Have for Each Client

Another constraint on your production is the minimum level of business, or revenue, you require from each client relationship. Remember, it's not the account that matters, it's the relationship and the revenue it produces that matters.

Production = Number of Relationships
× Average Production per Relationship

Notice that assets are not in the equation. Usually, in most managed money businesses, assets under management are a key component and production is correlated to assets. It is shortsighted, however, to see the world exclusively this way.

A client could have 30 accounts or just one. It's possible that a client may have no assets because the client is a hedge fund, so none of the assets are with you—they're at a Prime Broker—but the client does $150,000 in business with you annually. Again, this is where many firms make a mistake in connecting compensation plans to your asset levels. What does it matter if you have $600 million in assets if you do only $600,000 in revenue? What about the guy who has no assets, 50 relationships with money managers, and does $4 million in annual revenue? Why should he be punished for not having any assets?

Bottom Line: If you're going to get to $2.5 million in gross production, you need 50 clients who will do $50,000 annually with you. When considering a new client relationship, look at everything that surrounds it and estimate how much of the business you have to capture in order to reach your minimum target. Then be realistic about the probability of your capturing a significant percentage of their business. If a client does $100,000 annually in total gross production with three or four relationships, can you realistically capture 50 percent of that business?

Setting Higher Requirements for Your Clients

I used to struggle to get to my number each year. I had thousands of accounts. My average account had to be around $50,000 to $75,000, and I worked like a dog. I took 300 phone calls a week! I left it behind. I walked from 85 percent of the book. It was really scary at first—but then I had a revelation one night. I realized that if I continued to try to maintain my current book, I wasn't going to grow. If I didn't grow, I was going to be miserable for the rest of my life because I wanted to be one of the biggest and one of the best. So my choice became simple. Be miserable for the rest of my life or take the risk and do things differently.

When I looked at it that way, I realized the biggest risk to me was in NOT dropping the book and going for the growth. Part of that process was learning that you have to set higher requirements for your clients. Approach it by requiring that your clients pay you a certain amount annually—otherwise you cannot consider them as viable prospects. If you take on a client who won't produce the required minimum, you're setting yourself up for failure. You will hamper your ability to provide the required higher level of thinking and service, you'll bring down your average revenue per customer, and you will fail in your effort to get to the top. Don't take my word for it. Look at where you are today. How's your current strategy regarding "who you'll take on as a client" working for you? I rest my case.

In the fact-finding, initial stages of contact with a prospect, ask the question of how much they pay the street, in total, for all investment related services . . . including consulting, reporting, custody, asset management, hedging, lending. Many clients haven't done this themselves and have no idea how much they are paying the street to have accounts at four different firms. It gives you the opportunity to show them areas in which they can save money, and it "opens the books" on their street business. Then you can play "let's make a deal." You can tell the client that you will work with him if they give you such-and-such business, and agree to pay a fee of X amount. Show the client the money that will be saved by agreeing to do this. Explain that this will meet your required minimum business threshold and promise your full attention. Beyond that, it is no secret that when a client focuses street business on just one or two firms, there are other benefits to the client. Even if it is just being shown opportunities that others never see, isn't that worth it? But there are more. A client who does plenty of business with the firm clearly has an advantage in having access to products and people others do not.

Once you've told the client the business you want, at that point, there is no negotiation. Either the client says yes or no. Don't budge. If the client asks for a break on the fee or doesn't want to deliver the business you want, then you can and should walk. Wish that client luck and say you hope he or she reconsiders and calls you back sometime. Move on. Tell the prospect that you don't negotiate fees. Provide a fair deal that will make the prospect an important client to you and the firm the first time. No games. No negotiations. Here's the price . . . the client can choose to either keep doing what he or she's been doing, or work with you. You're either seen as different and better than the rest or not. If he or she doesn't, you don't want the business anyway because you'll be constantly having to justify your value to this client.

My mentor, Frank Rimkus, once told me that people only stay together if they are getting something out of the relationship. He said this applies to personal relationships as well as business relationships. At the time, being something of an idealist, I thought it sounded pretty cynical. But now I see that what he said is true. Think about it. Why is your wife or husband with you instead of someone else? Answer: Because he or she is getting something from you that is needed. Could be money, love, sex . . . or any combination thereof. You may share a common past . . . and that common past provides your mate with a level of needed comfort. "I couldn't ever leave John; he just knows me like no one else ever could."

Your clients have needs, and they are with you because you fulfill them. Be intelligent about knowing what their needs really are. There are clients who will stay with a financial advisor or money manager that is doing horribly year after year. Doesn't make sense from a purely clinical business standpoint, does it? No. But what the client needs and gets from the relationship may not be investment performance. For many older clients, being able to have someone there who is trustworthy— someone they know who will take care of their spouse and/or children if they should die. To them, this is more important than performance. For others, it's a level of contact that they like. "Fred calls me every week; we talk about the market and my account, and I like that." Some people want someone who is entertaining or funny. Most people want someone honest, whom they can trust, who brings them up, makes them feel good, lets them know that their account is important, and makes them laugh once in a while.

I recently had a prospect introduced to me who had $70 million in equity assets at another firm. They charged him no fee for the account because it was in ten stocks that his family had accumulated over the years. But now he had some specialized needs such as derivative-based lending and hedging. He needed top flight advice, guidance, and execution—and he needed it fast. He wanted to do a deal in one week and needed all the work done before that in order to make it happen. I made him an extremely competitive offer to manage the entire account for a flat fee and execute for him. The prospect immediately told me I was 10 basis points higher than everyone else. First, I knew he was not being truthful because I knew the market, and I knew I was actually at the lower end of the market—perhaps even below it. Second, I knew after meeting him several times that this was just his style.

During a business lunch, he stated, "I'd hate to see you lose this business for 10 basis points." I shot back, "I'd hate to see you lose *me* for 10 basis points." He asked if we could compromise. I told him no, that both he and I knew I was low on the fee and that I didn't want to play games. I was more interested in getting started on his issues and handling the many details that needed to be dealt with immediately. He stonewalled me. I paid for lunch and walked. He e-mailed me. I told him I was busy taking care of something for a client in another city and that I would get back with him in a week or two. He e-mailed me immediately. "I need you to meet with me tomorrow to talk." I told him I would be willing to see him in my office before 11:00 AM—but he would need to bring signed paperwork to transfer the account. He said he would.

The next day, he showed up at 10:40 AM. The receptionist called and announced him. I sent my assistant out to meet him with instructions that she needed to go into the lobby, take him to a conference room, and ask him if he had the signed papers with him. If he did, she was to take them from him and bring them back to my office. If he didn't, she was to excuse herself and come and see me. He didn't have them. He obviously wanted to waste more of my time and play more games. This is not acceptable. I told her to go back to the conference room and give him a note I had prepared for him. It read, "Thank you for coming in today. I appreciate that you want to do business with us; however, as we discussed, I have some matters to attend to with an existing client. I would be happy to take my attention away from these matters for a few minutes if you will sign the attached paperwork where marked, as you will then be my client. Otherwise, I regret that I will have to address your issues as time permits in the future." He left . . . and, just for the record, didn't get the work he needed to get done in order to make that deal.

The guy continues to e-mail me to this day. He'd never had anyone deal with him this way. He was so used to people falling all over themselves to get some little piece of his business that this was a whole new experience for him. He even flattered me by saying he respects the way I do business. I continue to tell him that I will be happy to work on his behalf as soon as we receive the appropriate and necessary paperwork.

The most important lesson in this is that I protected my time. I had invested what I thought was enough time in helping this man. He had been referred to me! He called *me*. I didn't go after him. I had been extremely generous with my time, my proposed fee, and my ideas—I wasn't going to give anything else away. At a point, it becomes his turn to step up and do business—or not. The saying goes, "Yes is best, no is OK, but maybe is not acceptable." Draw a clear line between clients and prospects. *Clients* are very important people. You have a special relationship with them, and special obligations. *Prospects* are entitled to exactly what they pay you . . . nothing.

Look at it this way. If you're going to live up to your goal of providing the client with a higher level of thinking, of delivering creative approaches and solutions to financial situations, and of doing a job you can be proud of, it is going to take time. Your time is valuable, because you only really have five assets: time, ideas, experience, reputation, and clients. Make sure you get paid for your time. Learn how to hold back with prospects. *Clients have a right to your time, prospects do not.* Prospects only get to hear your best thinking, your best ideas, and receive your full attention *after* they cease being prospects and become clients. There is only one way they do that. All it takes is a signature and a wire transfer of assets. Don't be confused; it is that simple.

It's unfortunate, but there are people out there who will pick your brain, get your best ideas and solutions, but have no intention of doing the business through you. Describe the end result of what you do, and keep the vehicles and methodology you utilize a secret until the prospect commits. Remember, a commitment is a signed paper and a wire transfer, not a promise.

In order to maximize the return on your assets to the firm and your family, you limit the number of client relationships you have and choose them judiciously. Strive to take on only those relationships that will pay you $25,000, $50,000, $100,000, or more in annual production. For your time, you cannot justify anything less unless you think it will lead to the necessary numbers within 12 months. Don't fall into the trap of qualifying someone on his and her assets. Remember, assets don't pay you, commissions and fees pay you. It's more important to find out how much the client pays the street each year in total and how many active relationships he and she has.

Many times people chase a prospect who has a total of $5 million, but who has no intention whatsoever in giving it all to you. Even if you do a great job and land the client, he'll give you $1 million, or $2 million—which, under many circumstances, doesn't qualify. But because of all the work you've put into the sale, you'll be tempted to accept this prospect as a client. This, of course, lowers your revenue per client, your performance, and gets you further from your goals.

Pricing Your Services

Basically there are three ways to go about pricing yourself as a financial advisor, broker, or planner: 100 percent fee, 100 percent commissions, or a combination of the two. What matters most is that you demand adequate and substantial payment for your services from each client before you take them on. If you are carrying some clients on your books now that do not meet the minimum levels, you have to replace them with clients that do meet the minimum payment standards. One way to do this is to actually convert that very client into a higher paying customer by sharing with him what you're doing. Be honest. Tell him that you're going to have to tell him goodbye unless the two of you can figure out a way to do more business together. Tell him that you don't want to lose him as a client, but that less is more, and that the firm wants fewer clients that do more business. You'll be surprised at how many step up and transfer in accounts from other firms. You'll also be surprised at the ones who transfer accounts out. It happens, but don't get depressed for goodness sake. They did you a favor. They really never liked you that much, and they weren't really clients you wanted. Trust me. They were trouble waiting to happen, you just didn't know it. As they transfer out, you should call them and thank them (not really, that would be poor form, but you know what I mean). As you replace clients, you remove clients. *Replace* means that you substitute one thing for another; something is eliminated and something else takes its place. Some of us just add new clients and call that replacement. Don't be confused. This is OK until you hit the 50 relationships level. After that, you must *remove* as you add.

If you are in front of very large pieces of business, you will begin to see that the business is being quoted in basis points. In order not to sound like a rookie, you need to know what the levels are for certain pieces of business. For example, if someone is liquidating a very large stock position, the client is probably sophisticated and will want you to quote him based on the national value of the trade. Certain factors come into play in this type of situation. If the stock is very liquid, then your pricing has to be lower. It's easier to move. If the trade would take a few weeks because liquidity is not high, the stock has high volatility, and it is traded on a foreign exchange, you can get paid more. Much more. There are a limited number of firms and limited numbers of individuals that can do the trade and do it right. Less competition. It takes a more artistic touch to move large positions like that without moving the stock all over the place and ultimately hurting your client. The same holds true with large derivative transactions for either corporations or individuals. Your derivative desk will build in a price for the desk and for you in the trade, and the trade will go off net to the client. You just have to be sure you and the desk don't get too greedy and put in for too much or your net price to the client will not be competitive.

For typical asset management business, you can be the best judge of what works and what will win the client. You'll probably find that the best clients don't usually pick the cheapest vendor for their more straightforward asset management business, so don't be too cheap in your pricing. In fact, you may actually find out that if you present yourself as someone at the high end of the pricing scale, and make no apologies for it . . . that approach actually appeals to some people. The world is going to fees in this area, so charging commissions to run a substantial account is truly not going to work long-term for you in most cases. What I've observed is that the really truly huge producers have some combination of fee and transaction income . . . because there is no way to charge an asset management fee on certain pieces of business. By their nature, they are transactional and must be priced as such. Fee business has its place and so does the transactional commission.

Practice and Rehearse

Charles Roth, professor, Wharton School of Business, said, "The price of success is constant rehearsal." Great athletes, entertainers, musicians, business executives, leaders in every field have a routine set of things they do every day. The difference between them and you is that they actually do it all the time. They practice championship technique every day, and they work harder and smarter than you do right now. Cal Ripkin, Michael Jordan, Tiger Woods . . . they have and/or had a routine. They rehearse. They make it look easy during the game or match because they practice it 100 times a day before anyone shows up at the park.

Rehearse your pitches. Say them out loud in the car. Pick a topic and practice your pitch out loud. Practice responding to different questions. Role play with a partner or mentor or assistant. Close the door to a room and give a brilliant presentation to the wall. You might think this is silly—but the payoff is that when you give a presentation that has been well rehearsed, using phrases and words carefully designed for impact, you will own them. You will have impact. This won't be by accident. It will look to the client or prospect like it is completely off the cuff and natural, but it is designed to produce the results you want.

Execute and Perform

Here is another difference between the average producer and the Top Guns. Top Guns execute and perform every day. They don't lose focus. They don't get off track. They stay on task. They have a clear vision of what they want. Using MPR during the course of the day will help you stay on tasks that will produce for you. Whatever you have to do to focus yourself every morning on your vision, do it. Tape your vision, the outline of your business plan, a motivational or focus statement to your bathroom mirror. Whatever it takes. Just do it. If others think it strange or abnormal or try to make you feel silly about it, forget them. Do it anyway. You *are* going to be strange and different now, because you'll be performing at levels they never will. You operate on a different level now. Smile and ignore them. Do what you have to do.

Assess the Results and Make Adjustments

Track the results of what you're doing. For the first year under the Top Gun Producer Program, you may not see a radical change in your levels of production . . . you might even see a decrease in revenue for a time. You'll feel scared and question what you're doing. This is normal. Stay on course. Assess results at around six months into the program and look at what you have in the pipeline. Has there been a change in the quality of the people you're talking to? Is your sales cycle shorter? Look at who you're dealing with currently. Have you slipped back to working with the same old clients who take all your time away from developing the book you'll need to be a Top Gun producer? Have you dropped 70 percent to 80 percent of the book that is holding you back and filled the pipe with 5 or 10 Top Gun prospects? One new client under your new requirements will replace 10 or 20 of your old ones. That's the key to this whole thing. Fill your pipeline with 5 or 10 people that qualify under your new minimums and you are doing well. Closing these people isn't easy, and it can take a bit longer than a week or even a month. It shouldn't take a year, but some do. If you have 25 people in the pipeline who can each pay you $250,000 annually, what if 3 or 4 hit over the next 6 to 12 months? What if 10 hit over the next 12 to 18 months? Now you're doing $2 million to $3 million or more in annual revenue! This is how you make the leap. You know the saying, "Taking it to the next level?" This is how you do it. It really is that simple.

Between months 6 and 12 you should definitely feel the momentum beginning to build. You should begin to see the financial results flow through in about 10 to 15 months. To determine if you're tracking appropriately, use can use the following as a guideline:

Year	Time Frame	Production
First Year	0-6 months	40-75 percent of base year run rate*
First Year	6-12 months	75-100 percent of base year run rate
Second Year	12-18 months	100-150 percent of base year run rate
Second Year	18-24 months	150-200 percent of base year run rate
Third Year	24-36 months	250-350 percent of base year—12 months
Fourth Year	36-48 months	500-700 percent of base year—12 months

*Base year is your trailing 12 month sales.

These are general targets. They are based upon actual experience. Some people may experience a little longer time frame to build the momentum, others may see much faster results. However, if you were producing around $500,000 in your base year, the 12 months following the start of this program you should see production in the $350,000 to $500,000 range. This is good! Don't be discouraged if you only do $300,000! In months 12 through 24 the results should really kick in and you should see revenue in the $750,000 to $1 million range. In year three,

$1.25 million to $2 million. In year four and five, $2 million or higher. If you have a $2 million business now, you should see around $1.2 million to $1.5 million in that first 12 months. In year 2, around $3 million. Year 3 and 4 should see $4 million or more if you stick to the program.

The most dramatic success story I've seen was in year 2001. The advisor did $2.2 million in year 2000. He and I met, and he took about a month to review his situation. He followed Top Gun to the letter. He looked at his clients and he looked at his firm, and he determined what he did well, what he liked to do, where the strengths were in the firm, and he decided which clients he would keep and which would go. He'll tell you that he cut his book to the bone and that he was scared. But he went to all the clients he had left and told them his story. They responded. In 2001 he did over $6 million. He worked the same number of hours, but with fewer clients. He did a better job for them, and they rewarded him. He had time for his family. Today, he'll tell you he is happier than he has been in years.

Differentiate Yourself

How can you differentiate yourself? Differentiation can be as simple as speaking a certain way. Many of you have an engaging characteristic that has helped you differentiate already—some of you know what it is and some of you don't—it's just a way about you that comes naturally and people respond to it. Do you excel at a particular sport? Are you a championship level chess player? Did you arrange an investment banking transaction that they may remember, write a software program, speak a foreign language? Are you from the south, or Texas, or New York but living elsewhere now? You have a different way of speaking that many people like. Anything that is memorable, that will differentiate you in the minds of your prospects and clients is useful. It makes you special and memorable. It's not ego. This is a marketing job and you are marketing yourself. If you have done something to change the industry, even in some small way, it can give you credibility. Were you an Eagle Scout? A fighter pilot? An astronaut? What do you do now that's interesting? Everyone should look at their past and their present selves and find the things that make them special or different and use them properly to differentiate themselves from all the rest. Leave a good impression that sticks.

Sometimes simply having a process that is demonstrably successful over time is enough to differentiate you from the competition. Delivering a sophisticated, yet understandable, business plan to a wealthy client or corporate customer that you can show has worked for others can be powerful enough to get you the business. Why is this enough? Because most of your competition has no process and/or no experience. Very few people are in this business for more than five years. Most drop out in the first five years and only something like 10 percent last longer than ten years. Most people in the business have no real experience with wealthy clients or institutions.

When I was cold calling about 15 years ago in Los Angeles, I was leaving messages all over the place and nobody was calling me back. I worked with Garth Casper, a man who is probably one of the best sales and marketing guys I've ever seen. He was observing my futile activity and he stopped me one day. He said, "You don't have a name that people want to call back. Why don't you call yourself 'Dutch.' That's your nickname from now on. Leave the message, 'Just tell him Dutch called! Here's my number,' then hang up." I thought he was crazy, but I was desperate, so I tried it. His simple point was that a lot of top executives might think it was cool to call a guy named Dutch and say, "Hey Dutch—How are ya?!" Everyone wants to know a guy named Dutch. I had call backs from CEOs of five Fortune 500 companies in a few days. Now I've been nick-named Dutch for 15 years. Garth knew how these people think. His genius is in knowing how people respond to the simplest things on a visceral level. You need to know what concerns your clients and potential clients at this same level in order to get through to them. If you can get to that level of understand-ing, it will help you understand what it is you really sell.

Know What You Really Sell

What are you really selling? Some of you are selling a prod-uct, and the product is strong enough to get you sales if you go through the motions. Most of us are selling ourselves, our expe-rience, our ideas, and our service. This is the intangible sale. People who sell intangibles have historically been paid much more than those who sell tangible items . . . because it's harder. It's an art.

What we really sell is peace of mind, future financial security, trust, consistency of vision, a process, a plan of action, expertise, honest advice, truthfulness, insight. The medium in which we practice our art is the financial markets . . . that is our canvas, where we apply our art. We paint the best picture we can for the client with the paint he gives us (his money) and our brushes (our tools), which are the combination of our knowledge, experience, products, and processes.

When answering the question about what you sell, keep it focused. Don't try to be too many things to too many people. Make sure the products and services you choose to represent have a market and that you can sell into that market competitively. In other words, every product or service should meet the MPR test. High profit margin and lower risk to you and the firm . . . and there should be a high probability that you can sell it to enough people to have a robust long-term business.

Diversifying a Focused Business

It's easy for your manager to say to you that you need to diversify your business, but actually doing it right is hard. The balance between having too many areas of business and not enough is delicate. As salespeople, we tend to move from one thing to another too quickly and we tend to bite off more than we can chew. But diversification and focus *can* coexist in your business. First, most of you have spread yourself so thin doing 15 different lines of business, trying to be so many things to so many people. Dropping to 3 lines of business is a huge change and is tremendously focused compared to what you did before. At the same time, you shouldn't rely on just one line of business . . . it's too risky for you and your family. Three lines of business is a reasonable target.

One business line should be as maintenance-free as possible because one or both of the others will likely be time-intensive. It should be a Cash Cow. Look at the lines of business you've decided to represent after using the Boston Matrix shown in Figure 6.1 and ask yourself the questions we've put forth in this chapter. Are you happy with the lineup? Have you decided how to drop the 80 percent of your book that is holding you back? Have you handed the accounts back into management, or have you taken on a junior broker or associate to handle them? Have you handed them over to your registered assistant to handle from now on? Whatever you've done, as we approach the next chapter on prospecting, you'll see that you will need free time to find new clients every day and every week and every year until you have become a Top Gun producer.

The hardest thing in this profession for people to do seems to be to stay with a chosen line of business long enough to give it a chance to come to fruition. As I said before, we tend to go from one thing to another in a never-ending quest for the magic product or service that will make us successful. There isn't a magic product or service. You are the magic. Your ability to sell, your ability to get on the phone every day and talk to people you don't know, your ability to execute every day and be a leader for your clients. Now, if the world is telling you that you're not competitive in this area, over and over, and you stay with it, you're just being stupid. But letting some initial blow-backs or failures throw you off the business altogether and send you down another path is just as stupid. You've chosen the business lines carefully. Stick with them and let them mature and achieve some critical mass.

For example, let's choose some business lines. We know that simple asset management in equities and fixed income is a fairly "plain vanilla" business, widely used and widely needed. Plain asset management could be a Cash Cow business that takes a limited amount of maintenance time once the accounts are put in place. Maybe you combine it with a comprehensive financial plan. That's business line number one.

There are certainly a growing number of individuals who need exposure to hedge fund products for a portion of their assets. A managed hedge fund portfolio is another line of business that wealthy individuals can put in place. The fees are fairly significant to the advisor, and the risk-adjusted rates of return to the client have been extraordinarily good in the past. This may take more oversight, but it pays more than traditional asset management business. That's business line number two.

Finally, perhaps you love currency trading and have a natural inclination for it. You can add this third business line, trading currency for wealthy clients and doing hedging transactions for corporations that have international business operations. That's business line number three.

Taking these three lines of business, let's see what it will take to build a Top Gun business.

What this fictional three lines of business does is show us that, in order to go from $2.25 million to $5 million, you must

FIGURE 6.3   Building a Top Gun Business

	EQUITY/FI MANAGED ACCOUNTS	HEDGE PRODUCTS	FX BUSINESS
Assets	$100 mm	$50 mm	$500 mm
Average Fee	0.75%	1.5%	0.15%
Total revenues	$750,000	$750,000	$750,000
Estimated Clients Required	20	10	20
Average Account Size	$5 million	$5 million	$25 million average volume

Total Business Revenue: $2.25 million
Total Number of Clients: 50
Average Production per Client: $45,000.00 annually

raise the average production per client or add more clients. Because adding more clients is actually detrimental to your business, the best option is upgrading the existing client base, replacing the lowest ranking client with one who has an average production of $100,000. When talking to new potential clients, if you agree to accept a client who produces $10,000 in annual revenue to the firm, you have actually lowered the average production per client of your book.

What rational business person, who wants to grow business, would voluntarily add a product that would actually lower gross margins or so obviously defeat the direction of his or her business plan? By adding the $10,000 fee per year client, you are making a serious mistake, unless you can direct that client to your associate or assistant. Even then, in most cases, all you're doing is fooling yourself. That client will likely want your time, your thinking, and your expertise. You will spend resources dealing with that client, the same as if you had a client paying $150,000 annually. You go down that road and you lose. It's that simple.

CHAPTER SEVEN

PROSPECTING

You miss 100 percent of the shots you don't take.

WAYNE GRETZKY

Top Gun Prospecting Rules

1. Short sales cycle—90 days maximum

2. Fill or kill often—weekly if possible

3. Find internal sponsorship

4. One-on-one, one by one, face to face

5. Focus on high probability, prefiltered targets

6. No letters, mailers, or seminars

7. Find money in motion and dynamic situations

8. Adjust your comfort zones

9. Never stop prospecting

10. Never say no for someone else

11. Use the magic referral technique

12. Use e-mail carefully, but *do* use it

Prospecting is like batting practice. You have to do it every day to stay sharp and stay "on" your game. It keeps you competitive, alerts you to what other firms are doing, and keeps you in touch with the market—your customers and their desires—which changes as the economy, tax laws, or other factors change. The more important reason to continually prospect is to upgrade your 50 relationships every year so that your business continues to grow.

Tough Markets

When markets get tough, clients look for solutions. If you are constantly prospecting to upgrade your book, or if you are trying to build your first book of business, *tough times are the best time to prospect.* Clients are looking for a change, a solution to what hasn't been working for them. Get on the phone. Call people and talk to them. Although many of them will say that they have an advisor and don't want to talk to you, ask them to tell you honestly how things have been working out with this advisor. If they think about it for a minute, they'll probably have to admit that their advisor hasn't done such a good job managing their money—because most advisors do not. There is your opportunity to simply ask them for a chance to show them a better way.

Tough markets are often used as excuses for people in our business to explain their lack of performance. There is no excuse for a lack of performance, only a reason, and usually the reason is that you did something wrong or the client wouldn't let you do what you thought was best. Perhaps you were talking to the wrong people about the wrong product or service at that time. Maybe you were talking to clients about buying stock or stock mutual funds in the middle of a market meltdown. Not smart. During market meltdowns, you need to talk about safety and bonds and asset allocation models and risk control techniques.

Tough markets are when I get most excited. This is when the opportunity to grow your business is so big you can feel it in the air every day. You can taste it. You can reach out and touch it. The landscape is shifting, markets are in turmoil, the financial advisors are all moving from firm to firm, lots of people are getting out of the business—either being fired or retiring. What do you think is happening to all those clients? They're in play! Go get them. They probably haven't heard from their advisor in months, anyway. Go see them if they qualify. Sit down with them and blow them away with what you're doing for *your* clients. This is when you can get big *fast*.

Get in Front of Dynamic Situations

The perfect situation for a Top Gun producer is to walk into a room full of executives of a company and ask them what is on their wish list. What do they want to do right now that's going to drive success for them and for their company? What do they wish was different in their business? Then shut up. Take notes. They'll tell you what to do next. Some will say they wish their 401(k) plan or employee stock purchase plan wasn't so lousy. They wish the company had a way for them to see all of their employee benefits and valuations of various retirement plan assets online. Some wish they could raise $250 million in a convertible debt offering, or sell a subsidiary for $150 million and use the money to buy another company that fits better with the direction they're going. They may wish they could integrate all their cash management needs in one place or hedge their foreign currency exposure.

Whatever they say, take notes. These are the things you want to deliver on. You can bring the power of your firm and its people to a situation and solve multiple issues for them. Then you will have added value, which will differentiate you from nine out of ten people they see each day. Pretty soon, you'll be doing a lot of business with them. You'll have a reputation for being someone who gets things done.

You may hear them say they wish they had a really great senior sales and marketing person. They'll chuckle, thinking that this is something you can't possibly help with, but they may be wrong. You might know a really good senior sales and marketing person at another company who is looking for a change. You might know the best executive recruiter in the city. One call to him and you might be able to help them with this. Whatever it is they say, you want to try to figure out how to deliver something of value to them, even if it isn't directly related to your business. If you do, you simply show them you intend to deliver on your promise to add value to their business, to help it grow, in any way you can.

Never Say No for Someone Else

Can you think of how many times you have *not* made a call because you've made assumptions about the person or company you are thinking of calling? You think he won't be interested because: a) His brother is a broker, b) He has an existing relationship with another firm, c) He's 3,000 miles away, d) He's dealt with one bank for 15 years. The possibilities go on and on. We make up reasons not to call! You've said no for them . . . and you haven't even had the discussion. Even if you have doubts, *make* the other guy tell you no. Never answer for someone else. You don't know what is going on in their heads . . . at their corporation. If you don't make the call and ask, how are you ever going to really know?

One on One, One by One

Whatever your chosen area of expertise, narrowing your focus should narrow the number of highly qualified prospects that exist in that market. Once you've identified and prequalified them through a process—using a caller or calling them yourself—you *have to* get in front of them. This is when you go one on one, one by one, and pitch yourself, your methodology, your process, your expertise, and your firm's capabilities—to the prospect.

Nothing replaces the face to face meeting. Nothing. If I have to drive two hours, I'll do it. If I have to fly to another city, I'll do it. You have to be smart about it, but that's how you connect. You don't connect in seminars, you don't connect in a cold call, you don't connect by mass mailer or letter. Face to face, one on one, one by one. That's how we get it done. You're only looking for 50 great relationships. If you can close one in five that you meet, and all five are well qualified before you go, and you can get in front of two a week . . . in two years, you should be doing over $2 million. You will have met with 200 prospects, and closed 40 to 50 of them as clients. They will each be doing at least $25,000 annually in commissions or fees with you. It is that simple.

Comfort Zones and Rejection

Human beings have comfort zones and, by nature, don't like rejection. What the Top Gun producer has done is reverse this particular human condition. He thrives on doing things outside the normal comfort zones and has made rejection his friend. He cannot live without being rejected every day. If he goes two or three days and is not rejected, he knows he's not do- ing his job—he can feel it. The truly successful Top Gun sales- person who is successfully building a business really feels strange if he cannot say that he was rejected by someone each day. You must reverse the normal human condition of fearing rejection and begin to fear the absence of it.

Who to Call

I've called everybody obvious . . . Warren Buffett, Bill Gates, Larry Ellison, and just about everyone else on the Forbes 400. Why not? Nobody has a monopoly on a good idea, right? I even talked with some of them. Those guys will talk to you, because they also know there is no monopoly on good ideas, and you just might have an idea they can use. You just better have something pretty impressive to say. I'm not advocating you call these people. It's not a high probability call to make, and you can bet these folks have a contact at your firm already, but it's not *completely* out of the question to land one of these people. Of course, the *probability* of landing any on the Forbes 400 list as a client is very, very close to 0. I was just too young to know better.

One of the teams where I worked many years ago had heard about this guy in Marin County, California who had made a movie called *Star Wars*. His name was George Lucas, and he was making so much money it was staggering. This was a team of two women brokers. They went to his ranch—Skywalker Ranch—and they jumped the fence and headed for the house. Apparently they were able to talk their way into his house, sit down with him personally, and discuss what they had done for their other clients. A few weeks later, George Lucas wrote a check for $20 million and opened the account. Within three months, they landed Woody Allen, Lily Tomlin, and about three other writers and producers as clients. What these two ladies had done with George Lucas was inspiring. They showed us that there was no reason we couldn't call anybody we wanted to for their business. Nobody was out of our reach. We started experimenting, going to the local hot spots, and asking everyone we met if they knew how we could get in touch with Madonna. It took four nights, but we found someone who knew someone, and we got the number and gave her a call.

One of the biggest producers of all time is a guy in Atlanta. Many years ago, a certain media company owner in town, who also happened to own the baseball team, was beginning to really build some wealth. This stockbroker called and called the guy to no avail. Then he had an idea. He thought he'd buy season tickets for the baseball team and get close to him that way. It took him years to work his way down to tickets that were right behind the owner's box. He started a dialogue with the media mogul and eventually got him as a client! Now he's the mogul's primary wealth advisor. It's all he does. One client. A multibillionaire. This broker is no different than you and me in most ways. He doesn't have an IQ higher than ours, he doesn't have some magic method for investing money that is foolproof. He just developed a relationship, showed the client that he could trust him, and gave the client his best thinking. It was that simple.

Who you will call depends upon you and the business lines you've chosen. Ideally, you want to call people who have the ability to make a decision without a huge committee approval process, and you want to call people who have significant influence or control over large accounts, blocks of securities, liquid assets, money or trading flow, or other MPR things for you to do.

Find the Pain

One of my former associates, Mike Conrad, is a Top Gun producer, doing over seven figures for many years. Mike is the expert at what he calls "finding the pain."

Mike's approach is based on the thinking that if the person is seeing him at all, there must be something they are unhappy with or seeking and haven't found at that moment. Through the relentless use of questions, Mike uncovers whatever that is. Once he feels he has uncovered *all* of the areas of pain, he has found the key to the most successful approach in his presentation and his close. He knows what matters to the prospect right now. He shows the prospect that he has the cure for their pain.

Money in Motion

What you want to do is find money in motion. Look for people who have sold businesses, are retiring, are getting large bonuses, have sold real estate assets, have just inherited money, have just raised capital for their business, etc. Many of these people have had relationships for a long time with a financial advisor who has managed a relatively small amount of money for them for years. You, however, are the expert at dealing with larger sums. You can position yourself above the existing relationships. People getting large sums of money feel very strongly about the fact that things have changed for them. They are fearful of making mistakes. They are looking for guidance. It is a critical time for them and a perfect time for you to approach. They may never have been open to a new financial advisory relationship in the past nor will they be in the near future. But right now, they may be open to hearing new thoughts. They feel they may need a higher level of service, a higher level of thinking or expertise, greater than that which they have been receiving from their current advisor. These people are motivated by fear and need an advisor who focuses on risk control and is conservative. You can be that advisor.

Business Owners and Individuals

In general, if you do the obvious, you will meet with mediocre results. In terms of individuals, the guy who drives the Mercedes and works on the 50th floor of the highrise downtown and lives in Beverly Hills probably has no money. He's leveraged. He probably has 2 to 4 kids and 2 to 4 ex-wives. This guy has no money! *Do not call.* He will be nice, he will make all the sounds of a guy who will do big business with you, he will waste your time, but when it comes time to opening the account, he will ask, "Now, what's the minimum again?"

Call individuals who aren't obvious. The best places to look are out of the mainstream. If you want to do business with business owners, get in your car and drive to the nearest industrial park. Look for the big concrete building with a nice sign, lots of regular cars, and a Mercedes or Lexus. That's the owner. Sometimes it's a nice pickup truck. That's who you want to see. They probably make something weird you've never heard of, but they make a lot of them and they know how to take risk. They love liquidity, they are debt averse, and can make a decision *right now*. They're businessmen. They are busy and they need your help. They paid cash for their car, probably owe nothing on their houses, live in a nice but modest neighborhood, and have $2 million to $5 million in the market and another $2 million to $5 million in CDs at the bank. You want them as clients now because after they sell their business, they'll have $50 million, $100 million, or more, and they will have a need for more complex services such as hedging and various tax strategies. Let them know from the outset that this is why you're talking to them now. Tell them they need to let you know when or if a liquidity event is being considered, because that is when you can really add value and potentially save them a fortune in taxes if it's done properly and you have advance notice.

We recently talked to a man named Roscoe who has a little company in the parts remanufacturing business. He has a small, but nice building, and the parking lot is full. The company is private and looks like it might do a few million dollars in revenue annually. When we profiled him, we found out he was actually the owner of 15 companies like this, and that this one company was worth over $15 million. Personally, he was worth over $60 million and around two thirds of it was liquid.

Early in my career I was cold calling out of a Standard & Poors Directory of Corporations. I came across a truck dealership, the owner was listed, so I called and asked for him. Clint, the owner, came on the line very quickly. He was very short with his answers, but courteous. Just seemed that he was all business. I closed for an appointment and he agreed. I asked when, and he said, "Anytime's okay—I'm here." This was too easy. The senior partner made me call him back and ask the financial qualification questions that I had forgotten to ask, given that I had been happy someone was willing to meet me at all at that point in my career.

Clint quickly understood why I was calling back, and said, "Son, if you're calling to find out if I have money, rest assured I do. This business is worth around $50 million, I owe nothing on it, and I take about $1 million a year out of it in pay." Clint became one of the best clients I've ever had. He was a gentleman, he was a business man who knew about taking risk, and he never wasted my time. If he agreed to see me, he did so because he intended to buy, not because he felt he had to or because he liked wasting people's time. Clint treated everyone with equal respect and dignity. They are out there, believe it or not.

This is where wealth exists in America. It's people like Roscoe who can write a check for $2 million or $3 million if they like you, just to get started. Roscoe can do $300,000 to $400,000 in business annually without much trouble. We're not his only advisors, but getting 25 percent of this man's street flow is $100,000. That qualifies . . . nicely. The wealth rests with the Clints of America, that drive a truck, live modestly, but are worth $50 million.

How do you meet these people? Everyone wants to be fancy about it. They try to network their way in to see the man through their accountant, attorney, and people at the club. That's a waste of time in my opinion. It's obvious, and people with brains see right through it. Just go visit the person. Sit down in his waiting room and wait. Go up to him when he's leaving the office, apologize for approaching him this way, and explain that you know he's on his way out, but that you really want to do business with him. Ask if you can see him early in the morning for coffee the next day. Be respectful, but show your true desire to have a real business discussion with him. He should respect that. If he doesn't, you probably just caught him off guard or at a bad moment. Tell him you realize your timing may be bad, and ask if you can possibly see him some another time. Don't give up if you have good intelligence that this guy does real street business.

Corporations

Corporations have a lot of ongoing needs, which are constantly changing. They have the need for investment banking services, cash management services, restricted stock services, retirement plan services, and on and on. You can find hotbeds of business in the financial officers and the human resource officers. These are the people who control the activity of the corporation's money on a day-to-day basis. They're the ones who decide who will execute on what services or transactions.

These people don't have time to fool around. For the most part, they don't go golfing and spend an entire day outside the office. They can't. They don't. They are in the flow of the lifeblood of the business, and they make decisions on a daily basis that can make or cost the company money. In order to reach them, you need to know what you're talking about, or you will quickly be categorized as a time waster—and be shut out forever. You need to quickly convince them over the phone that you can do something that is a bit different, and that you can potentially deliver an idea, service, or management style that they need, even if they're not aware of it yet. Assure them that their time will not be wasted, and what you have to offer is the kind of financial benefit that will impress their board members.

Prefiltering

Prospect for corporate and individual clients using Bloomberg. For those of you who do not have or use a Bloomberg, you are missing one of the greatest prospecting tools of our era. You can find out more information about a person or company in three minutes on a Bloomberg than you can in a day using any other means. This might sound like an exaggeration, but I promise you it isn't. These machines are, in my opinion, essential.

The Bloomberg cuts down on prospecting time because you can find the right people and contact information with a few keystrokes and get them on the line. You'll have their financial information at your fingertips. You'll know who owns the stock, who controls the company, who is selling stock, and what school that person attended. It is very robust, very informative. If you're not using a Bloomberg, then do the homework another way. Get the information off Internet search engines, business chronicles, etc. You only have so many calls you can make in a day. Make each one a high probability call.

If you can have a cold caller do your prefiltering and filtering, then you further leverage your time. It's important that you be spending your time doing what you do best. If that's being in front of people and making pitches, then you should be doing that. If it's managing money, then you should be doing that, but if your business is going to grow and you're going to continually refine your 50 to 100 relationships, someone else needs to be prefiltering, filtering, and bringing you up to speed . . . so that you always leave your office prepared.

The biggest producers who run their own money often have one, two, or even three people doing this prefiltering full time for them. They spend their time watching the money, making sure it's safe, and managing it. Those who outsource their money to other managers don't have to have all these salesmen working for them, but they do need a person who can oversee the operations while they go out and meet clients to review account performance, monitor the outside managers, and raise new funds.

Filtering

Filtering is simply eliminating those people who don't have the capability or willingness to do MPR business with you in the next 90 days. You can eliminate many people or companies before you ever call by prefiltering well. Know your high probability targets and focus your efforts during the work day on them.

Years ago, I was cold calling and surrounded by other guys who were cold calling, just like me. Some of them made 100 to 200 dials a day. They talked with maybe 50 people. If they were good, they might have booked one appointment for the senior guy or themselves. They focused on how many dials they made each day.

I usually made around 50 dials a day. I had 6 to 10 good conversations. I routinely booked 2 to 5 meetings a day. I didn't work the phones hard, I worked the phones smart. The hard work I did was in the area of making sure I did a lot of filtering before I ever made the call and making sure I had something to say that differentiated me from everyone else right away. Usually, it was something that showed I had done my homework before I called. A piece of information I had that wasn't well known. This was a tip-off that this wasn't just a cold call . . . I had done my homework.

For me, it just seemed easier to be prepared beforehand, rather than to find out what I didn't know afterward. I focused on how many quality conversations I had each day, not how many times I dialed the phone. You cannot stop meeting new, qualified prospects every day. If you stop, your momentum slows, your growth slows, you lose your edge, and you will fail. It may take time, but one day you'll wake up and realize that your business is worse than stagnant—it's contracting, dying a slow death. You're doing less each year, yet it seems you're working harder each year. This is the opposite of the results you desire, and the reverse of what you should experience with the Top Gun Method.

I see this every day, all around me, at every firm. A reasonably good producer for 10 to 15 years with a stable of loyal clients. He's doing $500,000 to $750,000. Everything seems to be going OK. He makes a good living, lives in a decent house, has a nice car, wife doesn't have to work, kids have nice clothes. He does nicely. In fact, better than just nicely by most standards.

Poor guy doesn't even know he's about to get flushed out of the business.

Let's go back to baseball. What happens to the guy who is paid well and hits .280 with 20 HRs and 80 to 100 RBIs a year when he has two seasons where he hits .230 with 5 HRs and 50 RBIs? He is sent to the minor leagues. Why? Someone else can fill his spot in the lineup who does better—or even just has a chance of doing better over the long term. This is the same thing, just a different business.

Every day I walk past a guy who sits at a crappy desk at a local bank. He's got all his little mutual fund brochures neatly stacked up around his desk. He's got his Series 7 license just like you and me. I'm so grateful I see this guy because every day I live in absolute fear—really terrified—that I might become him some day: talking to people all day long who have $200 about how to invest it. What motivation! This is our minor league system! Some of you came up through that system and made it to a high quality firm with sophisticated clients and capabilities. I don't know about you, but I don't ever want to be sent down to the minors. I've grown fond of life in the majors.

Get the Green Lights

On your calls with the prefiltered prospect, you're looking for what I call "the green lights." Each light is a test the prospect has to pass with a positive response or affirmative indication of some sort. Depending on what you're looking to market, the questions you ask will be different. For example, suppose you're looking to get cash management business. You call the treasurer or CFO of a company. The five "green lights" are:

1. Confirm the company has the minimum cash balances you require.

2. Is there an approved investment policy statement? Are they willing to fax or e-mail it to you? (This is a test of sophistication and willingness to genuinely do business with you.)

3. Are they willing to look at a new manager at this time?

4. Can they meet, face to face, in the next 30 days?

5. If they like what they hear, can they make a decision *either way* within 90 days?

If the prospect does not give you the green lights, move on. Maybe you put him in a tickler file to call back for another appointment if you feel he genuinely could work with you but timing is the only issue. Regardless, you must move on. You need to see people who are willing to consider a move *now*. We harvest the ripe fruit in this prospecting model, we do not store green fruit. The reason is simple: The ripe fruit is there, you just have to go find it. If you don't, someone else will.

You will hear plenty of people tell you of the value of getting in early with a prospect. This seems to be a noble thought. Building long-term relationships is a good thing. We look at it this way: Build long-term relationships after the prospect has made money, not ten years before. If we don't do it this way, we won't be around to handle that money once it's made.

You can fill the pipeline with guys who don't pass all the green lights and feel like you have a lot going on, but strangely, you're not doing any business! Isn't this fun? "Look at all the stuff I have going on, boss! I'm mailing stuff, I'm giving seminars on the weekends, and I'm cold calling out of the yellow pages all day and all night! Look at all my activity!" It's pathetic. No production! No fees! No actual clients! The few clients you have are pathetic. You are *confused*, and you will *fail. Grow up. Get tough.* Stop wasting time and money. Stamps are now 37 cents. The return on investment for mass mailing *is not there.* Demand more from yourself, your prospects, and your clients. *Pick up the phone and talk to people.*

Another example of getting the green lights: You've seen that a company has been purchased. You discover there are three or four people who will be receiving the proceeds. You call them. Here are the green lights:

- Are they rich? (Confirm what you've read.)

- Are they smart? (i.e., How much educating will I have to do?)

- Are they willing to *invest*? (Are they investors or depositors? We don't deal with depositors; we deal with investors.)

- Will they meet with you in the next 30 days to hear about your process and ideas?

Whatever the green lights may be for your business lines and however you feel best about phrasing your questions or framing the conversation, you need to have a feeling that this is a high probability target before you spend your time, talent, and energy. You don't want to give away some firm expertise in a presentation and meeting with anyone who isn't committed to coming on board. The German ace, Gunther Rall, who established the basis of what is today called aerial dogfighting, had a set of rules that he developed in World War II, which are used even today. One of these rules is, "never fire unless at close range." Translated to what we do this means, "only spend time on high probability cases that will pay your minimum required amount." You only have so many bullets you can fire every day—*don't waste them.*

Whatever you do, don't set up an appointment or meet unless you've got the green lights. You run a high risk of wasting time. Sometimes you have to go with your gut and go into a meeting without all the green lights, but usually you only want to do this if you already know a lot about your prospect. If you know the prospect has multiple holdings and is very, very wealthy, it may pay to just go and see him or her. He probably doesn't give that opportunity to everyone, so just getting an appointment is a win. Even then, you still run the risk of wasting your time and his. It would be better, after the appointment is set, to have your assistant call to find the top three topics he would like to discuss. That way, you can be prepared with some information and creative thinking on topics that are of concern to him now.

CARVER

In Richard Machowicz's book, *Unleashing the Warrior Within—Using the 7 Principles of Combat to Achieve Your Goals,* he tells us about something the U.S. Navy SEALs use called the CARVER matrix. This is a no-lose method of assessing their targets. What it does is clarify which targets are important, and beyond that, which ones should be hit first.

CARVER stands for Criticality, Accessibility, Recognizability, Vulnerability, Effect on the mission, and Return on effort. What we want to use CARVER for is identifying which business lines to be in, which business lines to focus on building first, which types of clients we want to have in our book, and finally, which ones we should go after first.

- *Criticality.* How important is this (client/business line) to achieving my objective?

- *Accessibility.* How easily can I get in front of this prospect? How easily can I enter this business line?

- *Recognizability.* How easy is it for me to find this prospect? How easily is it for me to recognize what I need to do in order to be successful in this type of business?

- *Vulnerability.* How much effort do I have to put forth to make this a very successful business? What resources do I need? Does this business take a lot of people, a lot of money, or a lot of time, or what mix of the three?

- *Effect on the overall mission.* If I do this successfully, will I end up where I want to end up, or does this just get me part of the way there? How much closer will I be to my ultimate goal?

- *Return on effort.* What will be the return on my effort, and when will I see it?

The idea here is that we need to think strategically and tactically, like the SEALs. We want to go after high margin business that is easy to identify, requires a minimum of effort to get

119

FIGURE 7.1   Sample CARVER Matrix

Business Line	C	A	R	V	E	R	Total
Cash Management	5	5	4	3	4	3	24
Hedge Funds	3	3	4	3	4	3	19
Foreign Currency	1	2	1	1	1	1	7
Mutual Funds	2	3	4	2	5	5	21

in front of and close and maintain, pays us very soon, and gets us much closer to the ultimate objective and goal, whatever that might be in your case.

The Matrix

The way to use CARVER is to design a matrix like the one in Figure 7.1 for each of your desired problems. If you want to find out which business lines to utilize, put them all on the matrix and rank each one in each category. Total them up in the end and you will find out which one is most important for you to focus on, then the next, then the third.

For example, in Figure 7.1 are four lines of business set into the matrix. I have ranked each one, from 1 to 5, with 5 being the most important and 1 being the least important. Even though I thought the hedge fund business was the most important business for me to focus on, it's really the cash management business. This kind of matrix helps you to determine which prospects, which lines of business, which clients matter most, as well as which clients, prospects, and business lines will have the most positive financial impact on our business with the least amount of effort.

There are reasons you have to be confident that there is a high probability of business for you and the firm before you go out to see people, even though you may miss a few opportunities.

First, you cannot convert everyone you meet to your way of thinking or your way of doing business . . . better to find out if there is a wide chasm between your two philosophies before you spend the time and money on an appointment.

Second, appointments are costly. Think of an appointment this way—it costs you and your firm money every time you walk out the door to a meeting. How much? If you're a $1,000,000 producer, it's costing you and the firm roughly $1,400 for you to make that trip. If you have to go to out of town to the meeting, it's going to cost you and the firm around $6,000 to $10,000. This includes the amount of business you will be giving up by leaving the office, either in commissions that you could be generating while there, or by making a better choice as to where you go for an appointment. Next time you think about going out to meet a prospect, think harder. Is it going to really be worth $1,400? Did you qualify the prospect well enough? What is the probability the prospect is going to do business with you? Honestly?

I recently went on a business trip. The hard costs of airfare, room, meals, cabs, was around $1,000. I was gone for two business days. If I am a $1 million producer, that's $5,000 a day × 2 days = $10,000. Total cost of the trip to the firm, $11,000. This is the third trip I've made to see people in this town. Now we're up to $33,000 in total soft and hard costs. If you use a commonly known rule of making three times your costs in profits, then I must expect to see at least $130,000 in gross revenues from these clients within the next 12 months in order for me to justify these trips. If I was going to see one client, I would want to see at least $130,000 from that one client. If we're talking about plain vanilla managed money, he would need a portfolio of around $15 million at about 80 basis points in fees to justify the cost of my trips.

Thinking this way will help you be a better businessman and show your managers that you think like they do, and that you are protective of the firm's assets, just as they are. If you do this, when you need them to go out on a limb for you, they will. If you need to spend some money that normally might not be approved, they'll approve it for you. Use your head. Think. Be smart. It's all about profitable business.

Keep the Sales Cycle Short

According to Charles Dwyer at the Wharton School, one of the key differentiators among salespeople is that *great salespeople consistently create a series of events to happen in a logical and timely fashion.* It is a fact, through studies that have been done by sales industry consultants, that salespeople with a shorter sales cycle have higher production and higher sales. The time it takes from the minute you've made contact with someone to the day he or she becomes a client, in the Top Gun Model, shouldn't take more than 90 days. Beyond that, the probability of the prospect becoming a client falls off dramatically. You need to fill or kill the prospect after two or three months. Tell him that you want to do business with him, but it has been your experience that after three months, the probability of your doing business is very low. Tell him you think he'll be making a good choice in deciding to go ahead and get started with you . . . can you stop by and get the paperwork signed and get started? If he sidesteps you again, thank him for the time and the opportunity to get to know him. Tell him you look forward to hearing from him when he feels he needs your skill and expertise. Then hang up, and forget him. Call someone else quickly. Get that guy out of your mind, off your contact list, and move on.

Why do we so desperately want to hang on to the prospect? Why do we continue to let a prospect pick our brains for free and get advice for free and service for free? Because we feel we have invested so much time and effort in the process with this person we don't want to admit to ourselves that it was time spent unwisely. Well, that's like buying a stock and not selling it when it starts to drop because you don't want to admit you made a mistake in buying it. A recipe for disaster and poor performance. Much better to apply good trading techniques and cut your loss now, then move on to a prospect with a higher probability of signing up.

Once you've made an initial presentation, if the business is not in the door within three months, don't count on it ever coming in. You may have another one or two meetings in that time frame, but just as a guideline, if the business isn't there in three months—move on. Sometimes as a final shot, think of a positive or interesting reason to call the prospect, and in the course of the conversation tell him you noticed that it has been three months since you'd first started talking. Mention that you've been doing this for a number of years now, and it has been your experience that if someone you truly wanted to work with hadn't come to the same conclusion within three months or so, it probably wasn't ever going to happen. Then ask what he thinks. You're just trying to get to the truth about where all this talk is going.

At this point, you'll get one of three answers. Yes, no, or maybe. Yes is very good, no is okay, but maybe is unacceptable. He'll either tell you he wants to move ahead with you, tell you that it isn't going to happen, or, he'll try to string you along some more. If he tries the last, he is really not the kind of person you want as a client. Actually, he is showing a blatant disrespect for your time and an unwillingness to be forthcoming and act like an honest businessperson. Explain politely and professionally that you've enjoyed the time you've invested with him thus far, and that he is welcome to call you when he feels he's ready to do business. (Talk is cheap, they say, but in your case, talk is very expensive—because it wastes your time.)

The facts are clear on this matter. Studies have shown the simple fact: Salespeople with shorter sales cycles have higher production—regardless of the industry. Don't be confused; it is that simple.

Going After Big Pieces of Business

You may, from time to time, run into what is called on the street "a piece of business." These are normally competitive bid situations with a corporation or other financial entity like a hedge fund or advisor of some considerable size. A hedging transaction, a secondary offering, a capital markets trade, a liquidation event for a treasury department, a block trade stock, or bond buyback are all pieces of business. This is the *type* of business that can catapult you to Top Gun status at your firm very quickly. Unfortunately, most average producers don't even know this business when they see it, and if they do know it, they have no idea how to play it. They blow it. The normal response of the average producer to this type of business is to try to come back with the lowest bid . . . because the lowest bid will win, right? Wrong. Absolutely wrong approach.

The correct approach is to find out what other pieces of business surround this situation, business that is coming up in the next few months. What this prospect is doing is trying to get you to bid for a piece of business so he can leverage your bid against the guy with whom he really intends to execute the transaction. Well, if that's the game, then turn the tables and get the trade . . . and more. He has to pay you to play in the game.

What I mean is this: You tell the client you want to bid on the business, but you recognize, as he must, that your bid has value. As such, what you prefer to do is find out about all upcoming business in the next 12 months, how much he has in cash for cash management, what the value of the stock option plan, deferred comp plan, or 401(k) plan might be. Once he tells you, you pick off the piece of business you want, and explain that you can make a superior bid to anything on the street, but he has to give you the trade, as well as the other piece you've selected. Oh, and you get the last look—i.e., the opportunity to enter the final bid or walk away.

So, if they have an existing stock buyback program, you want a few million shares of that, plus this trade. For example, if they have an outstanding bond that needs a rate swap, you'll do this piece and the rate swap, but not just one. The client gets a good deal for both pieces of business, which looks good to the boss, and you get not one, but two significant pieces of business instead of being used as a leverage against a competing firm for just one piece of business.

A critical part of all this is that you have to have a dialog with the desks that execute these pieces of business and be conversant in at least the rudimentary lingo, concepts, and pricing surrounding what they do. There will always be a low-tier firm out there willing to give the business away. The problem with them is that there is no assurance that they will stand behind the transaction. This is important. Any financial executive who does not know what this means needs to be told. What happens if the trade goes bad? What happens if there is an error? Who is going to step up and make it right? Is the low-tier player, with limited financial resources, going to readily step up and "eat" the problem for the sake of the integrity of the firm and its reputation? Not likely. Can you really be assured that the execution will be flawless if you use a low-tier player? What is the risk to the client if the execution turns out a year from now to be flawed—and it impacts the financials of the client organization? Will that other firm even be there?

Here's a real-life example: I was bidding on a plain vanilla stock option plan. The human resources (HR) person didn't particularly like me, and the senior executive had a broker at a competing firm to whom he wanted to give the business. I had done a number of things for this company, made a number of concessions, and delivered some hero-making ideas and transactions to them. This was their chance, in my mind, to pay me back for that work. I made a very competitive bid for the business, but I was one penny per share higher than the broker they wanted to give the business to anyway. The executive told me I had lost, and he got up to show me the door. I didn't get up. I told him that I had just one more thing to say. He sat back down looking exasperated and told me to go ahead. I said that his selected firm was third rate, that they weren't experienced nor staffed properly to handle this type of plan, and that for the one cent per share, he was making a mistake that could cost him much more than the combined pennies he thought he was saving. He told me to get lost. I did. I was furious, but I had to let it go.

A year later, that guy was fired, and the HR person told me that the selected firm had made some horrible trading errors and were unwilling to take responsibility for them. They were so bad that their own employees ended up suing the employer for failure to provide adequate executions. In some cases, the other firm took orders for stock sales but had failed to sell any stock at all! The third rate firm wouldn't make things right. All this over one penny a share! The moral of the story is that there is value in doing business with honorable people and strong financial institutions with integrity and capital. It often falls on deaf ears, but it is so true.

Internal Alliances and Sponsorships

Another thing the Top Gun performer does is get on the phone and find out who the critical internal people are who can help that performer do the job—the heads of the desks, the top people in the credit area, derivatives, cashiering, operations. Scheduling a trip, on your own dime, to see each and every one of them personally is a good idea. Send them a gift after you meet them, thanking them for their time. Tell them honestly why you're there. Let them put your face with your name so that when you call, they'll at least know who you are. Take them to lunch while you're there or bring them coffee or sandwiches.

It's not below you to show these people you have no ego about this. You need them. You don't want them to ever forget who you are. Find out about what makes them tick. Get to know them, and make notes about it. Send them cards and gifts and thank you notes when they go out of their way to take care of you and your clients. You have to understand that these people have so many opportunities for doing business each day that focusing on executing yours is the least of their cares. It is equally important to differentiate yourself internally as it is externally—perhaps more so. Here's a secret: The ones who can really save your butt when you need it are the ones that get paid the least and don't have fancy titles. I cannot tell you how many times in my career it's been the cashier or the clerk or the administrative person who can make a potential problem go away . . . or not—at their whim. If they think you're a jerk, *you* lose. Not them.

When you need their help, when you need them to pay attention . . . they will. Because you went the extra mile and showed them that you care about them. Some of these people can and do become your best life friends.

One valuable internal contact you can develop is the person who can introduce you into situations where big money is in motion. Whoever that is in your organization, you should try to develop a relationship there. In most firms, the investment bankers have a need for an internal broker they use at the firm, for regulatory purposes. Why not you? If you can get a dialogue going with a banker or analyst on a deal, then perhaps you can handle their personal account someday. If they get asked by a major customer, "Who do you use as a broker?" they can refer people to you. It happens. There is no better introduction in the world than having the investment banker introduce you to a man for whom that banker has just completed a $350 million deal.

Direct Mail, Letters, and Other Wastes of Time

If you want to reach out to wealthy individuals or corporate executives, direct mail, mass mailers, letters of introduction . . . don't work. They all spell failure. If you do this kind of stuff now and think that it's working, think again. Look at the time it takes, the expense, and who you end up with as a client. Now tell me that the return on investment—of both time and money—has been worth it. Stop this stuff now. Stop wasting your time and your firm's money or your own money. Letters, mailers, and seminars all have the earmarks of a low margin business. High cost, low return! In other words, a very low return on investment. They are timely and costly to produce, difficult if not impossible to get approved by compliance, and costly to mail. Let me repeat, they don't really work! There are many "broker sales programs" that will be happy to sell you their program for $12,000, complete with letters or postcards you should send people in the mail. You don't need this stuff. It doesn't fit in the Top Gun Model. It will waste a lot of time—either yours or your assistant's. The time it takes to write a letter of introduction to someone, get it proofed, approved, mailed . . . can you imagine how many calls you could have made in that same time? Can you imagine how many executives you could have introduced yourself to over the phone or in some other target-rich setting? You're better off hanging out at the bar at Pier

66 Marina in Fort Lauderdale where everyone has an 85-foot boat and a $125 million portfolio and buying a round of drinks now and then! Don't be confused; it is that simple.

These time-wasting activities are like drugs. They make you feel good at first, but they're really killing you. The secret killer in these activities is that they suck you in and make you feel like you're doing something work-oriented, but you aren't making any money. You're not talking to anyone you can help. If you find yourself writing a great marketing letter, *stop*. Pick up the phone and talk to the person. If you fall into the direct mail or letter writing trap, you will fail. I guarantee it. Wealthy individuals and corporate executives do not buy serious financial services or do business with people they haven't met. They don't pick up the phone just because you sent them a really cool letter. It's just a fact. You need to see people one on one, one by one, face to face. Pick up the phone and call them.

One of my favorite pitches when I really need to have some fun cold calling is the "coming to see you/rich guy" call. I call the person. I get the person on the phone, and I tell him that I'm a managing director of (super-duper investment company) and that I'm coming to visit. He always seems to ask me why. I then say, "Because you're a rich guy, and you're successful, and you're busy—and that's whom I do business with." Then he asks me who it was that told me he was rich? I claim it was Morgan Fairchild or something—it doesn't matter—then I ask if Morgan was kidding me. "Was she lying—you mean to tell me you're not a rich guy?" At this point, often he'll tell me the truth. He isn't rich or that he is in fact rich, but that he has no intention of meeting me. Now I'm off to the races! Sometimes you get the appointment, sometimes you don't, but you always have fun.

Referrals

A referral is only as good as its source. If the source is an idiot, everyone that person knows is likely to be aware of that, and the likelihood is that the referral could actually harm your efforts. The reverse is just as dramatically true.

The best referral technique I've experienced takes a bit of prep work, but the payoff can be worth the effort. When you're in a meeting with a client, or even a good prospect, pull out a one-page sheet of paper on your company letterhead with a list of names on it. On the list will be the names of people you and your assistant have prepared that you think the client might know from boards of directors, charitable organizations, the officers of the banks he or she works with, members of the same country club, people who have big boats docked in the same marina. *Make sure the prospect's name is on the list.* You present the list and state that your firm has targeted these people as people you think we should have as clients. "As you know Bob, we're not looking to do business with everyone. I can only manage 50 relationships. That's all. Here's a list the firm has come up with of people we think I should consider getting in touch with here in your city. Do you know anyone on the list?" Then shut up and make sure he has a pen.

This is one of the most amazingly effective things you'll ever experience. Everyone starts circling names and making comments about the people on the list. "He has no money, it's his wife's money. He's broke—lost it all in the commodities market. He's huge—if you can get him you won't need me for a client. He has no liquidity—it's all tied up in a huge real estate deal.

This guy is a jerk." It is truly beautiful. Take the paper back and thank him. Put it away. Don't mention it again. In fact, change the subject. What he just gave you is golden. You can take it back to the office and determine how to approach these people later. You may want to use his name, and if you do, ask permission. You may decide it would be more effective to go in blind. But now you know who to call, and you have a reference in their sphere of influence.

Another effective way to get a referral is to ask for help. Anyone who likes you even a little wants to help you. This is called "enrollment." Simply state the following:

"Bob, you're one of my best clients. I really like working with you. As you know, I am building a boutique practice here of no more than 50 high quality relationships and I'd like your help. I'd rather not spend my time looking for additional high quality clients, I prefer to spend it thinking about how I can be making or saving you money. I have room for two or three more clients, so if you happen to think of anyone you think could use my help, I'd be very grateful."

Advisors

Accountants or attorneys can be great sources of clients. You can develop a network of accountants and attorneys who can send you so much business you will never have to cold call again, and do millions of dollars annually in business. This is rare, however, and it takes time to build the network and relationships that produce results. Most firms don't allow you the luxury of two or three years to allow these contacts or relation-ships to pay off, so if you want to include this method in your model, you'll need to do the same things the rest of us do while you build that network. That means cold calling, getting the green lights, going face to face, and closing business.

I haven't had the same success with advisors. I find them to be terribly frightened of being held accountable for the results that I might produce, or fail to produce, and I cannot blame them. After all, they don't want to lose a great client because of something I may have done, particularly when they haven't even been paid to take that risk. But some brokers have figured out the advisor game. What they have done is earned the trust of the advisor and shown him and her that the business they do enhances the advisor's relationship to the client and has lower risk characteristics. These brokers have developed the relation-ship with the advisor over time and have shown the advisor how he or she makes money by including you in the process.

What has happened over the last five or ten years, however, is a trend for these firms to try to broaden their offerings to their clients to include high net worth consulting services. This is directly competitive to what we do. Many of the accounting firms that would naturally be sources for referrals have become our competitors, just as the banks have become. They are much more entrepreneurial that they were ten years ago. They have investment advisory businesses attached to their tax busi-nesses. Why do you think American Express, which has a huge financial consultant network, is buying up independent CPA firms across the country? Their vision is to handle all the tax *and* investment business for the client. Often the advisory depart-ment of a large accounting firm will design the strategy and plan for the client, then execute it through your firm's desk on a wholesale basis, thereby cutting you out of the equation entirely.

For that reason, once you've landed a client, you want to work with the client's advisory network and make sure they see you as someone to whom they could refer other clients. But, the Top Gun producer doesn't rely on advisors or referrals to deliver clients. You go after the client directly, one on one, one by one, face to face.

E-Mail—Reaching the Hard to Reach

E-mail can be extraordinarily effective if used correctly and with sensitivity. Because of the nature of e-mail, you can approach, and the prospect can come back to you thoughtfully, on his or her own time. It's noninvasive. So many executives today are e-mail oriented that reaching them this way is easier than calling—and they are conditioned to respond to e-mails. You can access people you may never get on the phone, and start a dialogue that way. You must be considerate in the approach, and a soft approach is the only way to go here. No selling, and be cautious of regulations.

"Pinging"

Use e-mail to "ping" on customers and prospects. Any guide to e-mail usage will tell you that a direct sales pitch in these e-mails is a big mistake. You want your lists to group people into similar interest categories. For example, all CEOs and chairmen in one group, all EVPs of Sales and Marketing, Senior VPs of Sales and Marketing, and sales professionals in another. CFOs, treasurers, controllers, CPAs in yet another. If you work deeply within industry verticals, you will group them into those verticals such as software executives, telecom executives, and deliver appropriate information to their businesses.

The e-mails you send should be geared to provide them with timely information that is right down the middle of their professional or personal financial interests, and not fluff. It should be something that shows them that you know what they live and breath every day. It should be cutting edge, in terms of timing and informational content, and it should be something that, when they read it, they will say to themselves, "This is cool." You want them to be able to copy it to others in their company or use the information in an upcoming presentation or discussion. Frequency has to be approached with delicacy. Not too often but often enough to keep your name in front of them.

CFOs and treasurers and financial professionals are concerned with tax information as it relates to financial reporting. They are concerned with getting the safest, but best, rate of return on the company cash and other assets. They like innovative thinking in the financial or accounting arena. They want to be kept up to date on new accounting methodologies and FASB rulings. An e-mail weekly with rate information comparing money market funds to commercial paper rates is a suggestion, as is an alert when the fed lowers or raises interest rates and FASB updates.

CEOs, merger and acquisition executives, and business development executives are interested in information as it pertains to the direction of their industry. They want to be on the cutting edge in terms of where their industry is going and seen as visionary and instrumental in the strategic direction of their companies. Any major acquisitions or strategic announcements from leaders in their industry should be delivered immediately without comment from you as to the implications. You may want to ask them what they think the impact to their industry might be. Solicit an intelligent response from them. Get a dialogue going. It can lead to business for you, but your e-mails cannot seem to be overt solicitations of business. That's better left to face-to-face meetings or to the phone. Keep one thing in mind—you can learn a lot more from them about their business than you will ever teach them. Don't preach to them about their business; ask them how such and such may effect their business. Learn from them. They've forgotten more about their business than you, or even your firm's analyst, will probably ever know.

In any case, the e-mails you send should be infrequent, perhaps one a month or two at the most, but each one should have impact and be seen as important. The instant someone thinks of your e-mails as tedious or noninformative, you've defeated your purpose.

Every three to four months, when things get slow or you're frustrated there isn't enough business happening at the moment, try sending an individualized e-mail to everyone on the ping list. Write, "John—just checking in—give me an update when you have a minute." Send out 100 of these and you'll be surprised. The phone will start ringing, and you'll do some business and get the momentum going. If you see an article or announcement about something great that someone or someone in their company did, send an e-mail with "Congratulations" in the subject line. Sounds corny, but have you ever failed to open an e-mail that says, "Congratulations" on it? There's a 100 percent chance it will be read.

CHAPTER EIGHT

VIRTUOUS SELLING

You have to perform at a consistently higher level than others. That is the mark of a true professional.

JOE PATERNO

Top Gun Rules of Selling

1. Be prepared to close from the first minute of the first meeting.

2. If prospects won't do business with you within 90 days, forget them forever.

3. Tell stories to illustrate your key points.

4. Differentiate yourself in some way.

5. Give prospects more than one valid, logical reason to do business with you.

6. Figure out how you can make them heroes.

7. Ask them what's on their wish list.

8. Remember, it's about them, not you.

9. Make promises—and deliver.

The Top Gun selling approach is based upon the Virtuous Selling concept. It's named Virtuous Selling because it is focused on doing what is right for the clients first. It focuses on their concerns, their desires, and the people *they* want to impress. When you sell virtuously, you look for ways to make heroes out of the people you are dealing with as your clients. It is that simple.

In reading the dictionary definition of virtuous you will find that virtue has a number of words associated with it; courage, bravery, strength, purity, morality, power, and *potency*. It's interesting that with this one word we can see that doing the right thing for your clients can have a strong and powerful result in your life and success.

If your efforts are concentrated on finding out who your client's people are—who he or she reports to or needs to impress, and who is important in his or her life—you accomplish two things. First, you get to know your client. Second, it helps differentiate you from almost everyone else the client is working with because the rest don't care in this way. They only care about what can be done for them. You care about figuring out how you can make the client look intelligent and creative to the people that mean something to him or her. If you work hard to make the prospect or client the hero, and stop focusing on yourself and what your needs and desires may be, you will find that your needs and desires are fulfilled. Why does this happen?

If you deliver something of value selflessly and focus on making your client or prospect a hero to the people who need him or her to be one, the client will figure out a way to work with you and pay you well for your services.

Don't Be Confused about Who You Are

As we talked about earlier, a mistake people commonly make as they become successful in this business is to believe that they are money managers, traders, investment bankers, analysts, etc. There are people in the world who are better money managers, traders, bankers in their sleep than you or I will ever be. You and I are salespeople. You can call yourself a financial consultant, financial advisor, money manager, investment banker, or whatever you like to the outside community, but don't be confused. More importantly, don't fool yourself. You're in sales. You're a salesperson. Selling is what you do.

Top Gun salespeople are highly trained, sophisticated, experienced, consultative experts in the financial field . . . and they charge for that expertise when they land a client. They are proud of who they are and what they do. You should look at what you do and know that it is essential, it is important, and it is valued. Before you can show anyone how to protect their assets, how to avoid paying too much in taxes, how to create and manage a well balanced investment account that will stand the test of time, you have to land them as clients. You have to sell them on yourself. Selling comes first.

Next, in order to get your clients to move money the way you feel it should be moved, you have to persuade them. You have to sell them on the fact that your ideas, connections, and services are trustworthy and are *always* in their best interest. So, sales also comes second. When the market gets tough and people aren't making money, and you have to go and hold their hands and get them focused on the process and your long-term plans so that they'll stick with you through tough times, you are selling yet again. We all sell all the time.

Also the bigger you get, the more selling you do. You never get promoted out of a sales job while on the road to success. The CEO of a company has to sell customers, shareholders, Wall Street, and his employees on his vision. He's selling to virtually every audience met, in virtually every meeting attended. The best CEOs are the best salespeople. They're the ones who are nothing less than passionate about what they do and what they have to offer.

Author Robert Cialdini has written a number of books on the topic of persuasion, specifically, the psychology of persuasion. He delves into the psychological and social factors behind peoples' decisions. In the October, 2001, *Harvard Business Review* he published an article entitled, "Harnessing the Science of Persuasion," where he outlined how powerful the art of persuasion can be. Some people are naturals at this, but what about the rest of us? What about those of us to whom "people skills" are not natural or easy? Cialdini states that persuasion can be broken down into a science that is governed by principles, just like anything else. Basically, he states that people do things for the following reasons:

- *They like you.* The way you utilize or apply this principle is to uncover real similarities you have with your prospect and offer genuine praise.

- *Reciprocity.* People feel a natural need to repay you in kind for value you have delivered to them. The application is to give what you want to receive.

- *Social proof.* People follow the lead of others. The application is to use peer power whenever possible.

- *Consistency.* People align themselves with their clear commitments. The application is to make their commitments public, active, and voluntary.

- *Authority.* People defer to experts. Expose your expertise; don't assume it is self-evident.

- *Scarcity.* People want more of what they have less of. The application is to highlight the unique benefits and exclusive information.

Cialdini touches on a number of Top Gun principles. Specifically, his principle of Reciprocity is central to the Top Gun Model. The entire reasoning behind the Top Gun principle of making heroes out of others through virtuous selling is to develop a pipeline of prospects and clients who continually have the desire to repay you in kind.

Cialdini's principle of Authority reminds me of a meeting I had as a young salesperson with a very wealthy and seasoned investor. In my presentation I had discussed a number of my prior accomplishments. Then, realizing that this may sound pretty silly coming from a 20-something kid to a 50-something man of significant accomplishment, I stopped and apologized for going on about my accomplishments. He cut me off and said, "Hey kid, don't apologize. I wouldn't buy anything from anyone who didn't blow his own horn a little bit. It's important that I know what you've done and that you have confidence in yourself."

We use Cialdini's Scarcity principle as a cornerstone of the Top Gun Model in only allowing 50 client relationships. Psychologically, by establishing this limit formally within our model, it becomes real to us—and therefore to our prospects and clients when we talk about it. For years, advisors have told us to say things like, "I have a limited number of clients," or, "We're very selective with whom we do business." This just sounds hollow, doesn't it? Well, it sounds like bullshit to our prospects and clients, too. But not when you're telling the truth. When you have authenticity to your claim of handling absolutely no more than 50 superior clients, making it to your book becomes appealing. In fact, by definition, this is what makes something valuable. The fewer the number of people who can attain it, the more exclusive becomes the club. It addresses the human instinct to be thought of as special.

When word gets out that you have a 50-client limit, it can help you in client acquisition through referral. Your existing clients will no doubt be asked by friends or business associates who they deal with in your area of expertise. They'll say it's you, of course, but will have to add, "He only handles 50 clients though. I'll have to call him first to see if he can work with you." This is powerful. The stage is set for you, and you haven't even received a phone call yet.

High Performance Selling

Michael Beck, author of *High Performance Selling*, is, like us, a salesperson. You can read his book in one hour, which is great.

Mark those chapters that particularly apply to what you're doing and what you need to do to remind yourself to do in order to perform at your highest level. Beck also understands the power of visualization, an important tool in the Top Gun arsenal.

Beck tells the story of a salesperson he worked with a woman named Jackie who loved to go to the Caribbean and lay on the beach. This woman happened to be a top performer. What she liked to do was keep pictures of the beaches she wanted to visit around her office, always in sight. When that last phone call had to be made, when handling the upset customer was necessary, when asking the tough questions and making the fill or kill phone calls each week were staring her in the face, Jackie made those calls. The beach was her motivation. She visualized the fruits of her labor. Picturing herself relaxing on the beautiful white sand, while the sound of rolling waves lulled her to sleep, probably gave her the incentive to keep going on the days when it would have been far easier to give up. Find a reward that you can focus on. Find your beach. Put a symbol of it where you will see it every day.

The Top Gun producer who utilizes time selling to the firm's strengths, and more importantly, by being consistent in the use of MPR, is able to recognize situations in which time is spent wisely. The more familiar he becomes with MPR, the sharper his instincts will become. He'll learn to recognize quickly which opportunities are not making the best use of his time and/or his firm's budget and put a stop to those conversations right away.

The successful salesperson goes and gets the sale, he doesn't wait for it to come to him. He engages in intellectually stimulating conversations with his prospects and clients about their concerns and their businesses. Using his natural curiosity, he frames open-ended questions that elicit real thoughts and feelings from his clients or prospects about their concerns and problem areas. From that discussion, the avenues for a successful sale are born.

The Top Gun producer provides solutions—with multiple options whenever possible. Sometimes it will become obvious that your firm isn't the *best* option at the time. Honesty is essential. If your integrity beeper is going off inside you, saying that this client's problems might be better solved by another firm, go ahead and suggest it. The top producers, the class-acts of the business, work to solve the client's needs first. It's always better that such a suggestion comes from you. You can always ask for the last look, a technique Beck calls "book-ending."

Find the Reason They'll Buy

There are really four basic reasons people buy *anything*:

1. Fear

2. Pride of ownership

3. Something they stand to gain

4. Imitation of others they respect

If you keep these four things in mind when you're in a presentation or meeting with a prospect, you can hone in on which reason motivates your audience. Once you've identified it, gear the whole presentation to that element. Wharton's Dwyer states, "Never expect anyone to buy unless you give them adequate reason to do so." Now, you and I hear this, and say, "Well, that makes perfect sense—everyone knows that—it's intuitive." If that's the case, why do so many salespeople expect prospects to do business with them *without* giving them several valid reasons to do so? How many times have you walked into a meeting and were not prepared to give the client an answer to the simple question, "Why should I do business with you?"

Simply stating that you are better, or will pay more attention is not enough. No one is going to make a major financial decision based on that one-sentence, hollow answer. You need to *prove* that you are better. You need to lower the potential, in the prospect's mind, for making a mistake by moving business to you. Remember, any change is perceived as being fraught with risk. You need to deal with that issue. What you want to do is find a way to show the prospect that the *real* risk here is in *not* making the change.

This can be accomplished by pointing out the looming hazards of staying put. Give examples of how you've successfully thwarted similar potential disasters for other companies. Get the prospective client to see that what you're proposing addresses every single item on his wish list, and *then* some, while his current situation does not. Explain that you consider it part of your job to allow him to sleep peacefully at night. He's the quarterback, heading for the end zone, and you're the guy out front blocking and clearing the way. The only logical choice is to make the change.

I recently had a meeting with a prospect and, before I went into the room, I silently rehearsed my "50 EAT" as I call it. This is my reminder of the four reasons I can give this person to do business with me. I only have 50 relationships, which allows me to deliver a higher level of thinking and service to my clients. I have 20 years of Experience, which means I've seen a plethora of ways money can be lost and know how to protect the future of his investment. I am Accessible to him and to the best minds in our firm on any subject he desires, which means he can make better-informed decisions. My clients Trust me because I act as their advocate in all financial matters. Fifty relationships along with Experience, Accessibility, and Trust. Four decent reasons to do business with me instead of somebody else.

Listen to the Music

J.P. Morgan once said, "There are two reasons people do things . . . the reason they state and the real reason." Over the course of a career, you will hear every excuse imaginable for not buying or not to move the account. The key to getting past these is what I call listening to the music in their words . . . looking beyond what they say is their primary concern. Often, you will find that the real problem is something else entirely, something you can handle. But, for whatever reason, the client is just not capable of communicating it directly to you.

I remember a big prospect I dealt with years ago. He had a large portfolio, was an intelligent person . . . he had many of the things I look for in a client. I danced with him in meeting after meeting, call after call, then even more meetings. He used every excuse not to act. The most frustrating part of this process with him was that I liked him and I knew he liked me. I thought we could really work well together. So, I finally took an old trust officer with me to help me get this account. I was simply stumped. We sat down and had a nice long chat. The trust officer asked a lot of questions, then finally, we left. When we got out to the car, he said, "Next meeting, son, make sure the wife is there. She's the one who calls all the financial shots."

I replayed the conversation we just had and remembered the trust officer asking a lot of questions about his family, his wife, etc. Subtly, the man had revealed the true essence of the dynamics within his household. He just wasn't comfortable with telling us directly that we also needed to talk to his wife. I didn't catch it because I was too focused on what *I* wanted to do with his account to hear what the man wasn't telling me. Thinking back, he had provided me with at least ten clues that I didn't pick up on. I wasn't listening to the music. Don't make that mistake. If you listen to the music, the song will come through.

The Presentations

Once you've got a meeting with the prospect, you should be prepared to make a two-minute presentation on who you are and what you do. It should move logically from your background, to your accomplishments, to your business principals, and then zero in on the processes you have that are appropriate for people or companies like the prospect's. They need to buy into you, your process, your business principles, and your philosophy. These are important issues. If you get resistance, or are asked to compromise at this stage, it is time to cut the meeting short, wish the prospect the best of luck, stand up, extend your hand, smile, and leave. You cannot compromise your process, your business principles, or your business philosophies. Ask any top producers and they will tell you that the only times they have ever gotten into trouble with a client can be traced back to their having compromised in one or more of these areas.

If the prospects do buy off on these things, you need to get them talking about their money and where it is. Find out what they want to do with their money and what they want it to do for them. Who have they talked to already? What ideas have they heard that were good? What have been their concerns and fears? Get all the information you can and pay attention. Listen to what you're hearing and also to what you're not hearing. Don't leave there without being clear on what they want to accomplish and what their fears are. Once you have all the information, you've got a decision to make. You either schedule a date to come back with a strategic plan of action for their approval or, if you feel enough ground was covered that the prospects are convinced that you're their person, go ahead and close.

It is here that you outline for them the next steps—here is where you draw them the clear path to a successful relationship. Now is the time to discuss the cost of doing business with you. Cover this up front. Better for you to find out quickly if this is going to be an issue. I deal with it by telling people that I never let cost get in the way of doing business with someone I really want to work with. I don't compete on price, but I'm competitively priced. We decide and agree up front on what the client will define as success in the assignment I've been given. I set up a meeting six months from the day they begin to work with me. On that day we will go over everything that I've done and let them decide if value was delivered.

If you have a second meeting prior to the close, reiterate what you know to be their goals and concerns. Then tell how you intend to deliver the former, while eliminating the latter. Place before them a carefully and thoughtfully constructed plan of action that is competitively priced. Give them multiple, valid reasons to do business with you. This is your second meeting. You are there to close. You should rarely have more than two meetings. Be genuine and give a lot of yourself at each meeting. Let the people get to know you a bit. If they cannot get their arms around who you are and what you're all about after two meetings, and they are unwilling to commit in writing to doing business with you, then you've got other people to see! You may miss some really big opportunities, but you won't waste a year or two of your life dancing with people who don't have anything better to do than to waste your time.

If all goes well, however, as it often will, there should be no reason not to feel comfortable asking the people in front of you to sign paperwork, write a check, or wire the funds. Remember that the deal isn't closed until this has taken place.

Positioning

In order to do the levels of business we're after, you cannot be trapped in the old model of calling 100 clients to get 30 to 40 orders for stocks or bonds or a mutual fund. It simply does not work in the Top Gun Model. You must have the ability to make discretionary decisions for the bulk of the book. If the money is outsourced or managed by outside managers, you must have the authority to make strategic shifts in asset allocation and managers quarterly, biannually—or less, if you deem necessary.

This helps you to close, believe it or not. As you are moving into the closing phase of your presentations, explain to your prospect that you do a large volume of business, you have to make a number of critical financial decisions for people every day, and you cannot be required to make 100 phone calls to ask for their approval. If you did that, you wouldn't be doing your job effectively. This means the client must accept a structure to the relationship that allows you to call the shots, based on an agreed upon set of rules and guidelines. This is crucial . . . it's a deal-breaker.

Generally, in the big asset allocation decisions, you *want* to consult the client and get approval. But, in terms of the issues that are bought to effectively implement the strategic allocation, you cannot be bothered with making those calls. Period. No negotiation on this point. Setting up the relationship from the start in this manner serves another purpose. It differentiates you from most of his other advisors and brokers. Most don't make such demands, which is why they are where they are, and why you will be doing ten times their production four years from now.

There is a very client-centered reason for structuring the relationship this way also. In times of opportunity, you need to move swiftly. Serious opportunities do not remain in the market for long and are sometimes gone in an hour or less. For example, I think General Electric stock was trading below $29 per share for just an hour or two in the days following the September 11, 2001, terrorist attacks in New York City and Washington, D.C. Within weeks, it had rebounded to $40 per share. There are thousands of opportunities throughout history that existed for just a few hours before they were properly repriced by the market and the opportunity was gone. If you have to call 50 clients and seek approval for this type of thing, you will fail. You will end up missing the opportunity for most of them, because the clients could not be reached. This makes performance suffer. Theirs, as well as yours.

Focus on Making Them Heroes

For every individual and for every corporation, the specific set of problems you will be addressing and selling to are different, and your presentations will be geared and tailored to those specific issues, but they all usually revolve around the same set of desires and goals:

Individual Account Desires

- Maintain wealth
- Pay less in taxes
- Take care of future generations
- Be "looked up to" by the family
- Make solid, informed financial decisions

Corporate Officer Desires

- Lower the company's expenses
- Achieve a higher net rate of return on cash safely
- Look good to their boss or shareholders
- Be considered "brilliant" by their peers and boss
- Show that they go the extra mile in their job
- Improve existing policies and procedures
- Come up with creative new ideas for the company
- Know what their competitors are doing
- Stay on top of the company's financial issues
- Make solid, informed financial decisions
- Be seen as fiscally conservative with company assets
- Be considered "in the know" about their business
- Show a high level of sophistication and knowledge in their job

In the sales process, your desires and needs are unimportant. It is the prospective clients who matter. The presentation isn't about you or your firm or how great you are: 99 percent of the presentation is about them, 1 percent is about who you are and how great your firm is. The meetings are about them, their concerns and objectives, what you can and will do for them, how you will do it, and what it will cost. A decision to go with you is a huge leap of faith. Faith that you will deliver on your promises. Faith that you will be there for them and not hide from them when the markets get volatile. Faith that you will lead them in times of uncertainty. Faith that you will tell them the blunt truth, even if it isn't pleasant, when they need to hear it. Faith that your firm has the financial strength to weather the storms, faith that your firm will execute for them properly and will stand behind their contracts and commitments. In order to ask for the business, you have to make them understand that they can count on you.

What is important about you at this stage is that you have an impact on your audience. You have to differentiate. You must have some presence. You must generate a connection. They must feel confident in your abilities and the likelihood of your delivering on your promises. You have to be confident. People equate, often subconsciously, confidence with competence. Right or wrong, they do. How do you make them feel as confident about making a decision to go with you as you seem to be?

Tell Stories

In sales manuals, they are referred to as "third party references." I just call them stories. But the stories you tell should be succinct, must have a purpose, and must be directly related to that person or the company's current situation. Show the prospects how one person or company you advised didn't take your advice, with negative consequences. Give real-life examples. Engage them in the story by asking if they remember something of interest (and relatable) that was in the headlines a few months ago. Tell them what to expect if they take your advice and do it right. Let them know how you hate to see wasted opportunities.

Show them how true wealth thinks. Shift their comparative base.

If you're dealing with people who are newly wealthy, they *need* to know how differently people of wealth think about returns on their money, about their kids, their charities, everything. They don't know. You do! They want someone to tell them how they need to think now. You work with wealthy people every day. Show them you've been there. Let them know subtly that you know people and families of wealth. These people work with you, they trust you as an advisor, and this is the way they think about money, investing, and returns. Tell them that they have a unique opportunity in time, something so special that it's almost sacred . . . the opportunity to change not only their own lives, but the lives of everyone in their family for generations to come if they handle things the right way. It is your strong desire to help them make that happen.

I have a story I tell to people who've made a sudden and large amount of money. I tell them about a man who had received $60 million in stock from a company that had purchased his little firm. We knew the company that had acquired his, we had done our homework, and we felt that there was no way this company was going to remain at this high level of valuation for long. In fact, due to certain market factors that we (and everyone else) knew about, we were fairly certain the stock was going down by at least 20 to 50 percent within the next eight months.

We advised him to hedge a large portion of the position, or to simply sell 80 percent of the position and diversify the proceeds after taxes into a broad balanced account. He told us that he thought this company was going to be the next Microsoft. That's when I knew we were in for trouble. I told him that I was very sorry, but that I couldn't work with him if he didn't take my advice and sell a minimum of 75 percent of the position. Well, the stock didn't go down 50 percent. It went down over 90 percent.

Today, the stock is worth perhaps $4 to $5 per share. His $60 million is worth $3 million, if that. Now, many of us won't feel sorry for anyone who has $3 million, right? Well, I don't feel sorry for him necessarily, but I do feel terrible that there was an opportunity to change many, many lives for the better that was lost due, frankly, to irrationality—to put it kindly. Think of all the charities he could have established. He could have established five foundations at $4 million per foundation and changed lives forever without hurting his standard of living at all. He could have given $20 million worth of stock to ALS research (Lou Gehrig's disease), or to AIDS research, or to Alzheimers research. Finding a cure for any of these things will prevent untold suffering around the world and help millions of people live long and fruitful lives. All of us have been touched by these diseases in some way. Think of all the people in his own family he could have provided for—now and into future generations.

Because he appeared to be a greedy person, I tried to appeal to his greed by telling him that the difference between a ten-year-old Learjet and a new Gulfstream V was in his hands. He didn't react to that either. Maybe I underestimated his greed. I don't know. What I do know is that to get a windfall like this man received, and to be so ignorant, . . . it's almost a crime, wouldn't you agree? But we see it over and over again.

Stories seem to be the most powerful way to impact people in the sales business. Stories are what we respond to viscerally because they are real. Stories are what we remember. This is why great books and great movies are fundamentally great stories. The greatest preachers and persuaders and politicians in history are the ones who can tell great stories. Stories move us to take action. People listen and remember the stories you tell them, but they often forget a series of facts and figures. Paint the picture for people with stories, you'll have an impact on them, you'll connect with them. They'll remember you, and they'll give you their trust and their business.

CHAPTER NINE

TOP GUN CLOSING STRATEGIES

When you win, nothing hurts.

JOE NAMATH

At the point of making a closing decision, clients feel very vulnerable. There are a thousand things running through their heads and emotions that are running counter to their saying yes. This is because there is perceived risk in saying yes and making the change to move the business to you. We need to delve a little further into the reasons why people buy. This is crucial to your existence in this business.

The Four Associations with Value

According to Charles Dwyer, author and Wharton Business School professor, there are four control factors at work surrounding the close in the mind of the buyer that will determine your success. You can substitute the word "success" for value or value satisfaction.

1. The *potential* for value satisfaction

2. The *probability* of value satisfaction

3. The *cost* of obtaining that value

4. The *risk* of not obtaining value

There is no magic closing technique or style. There is no magic phrase that will win the business 90 percent of the time. Every client responds to different things. So closing is a subtle art that takes time to learn. Some people like to close themselves. They come to you. Like a fishing lure that you "play" in the water, the fish chases and you move a bit, he moves a bit, until finally he bites, and you've got him. Some people like the hard sell and only respond to the tough finality of the fill or kill close: "You're either in or you're out—what's it gonna be?" Some people like the softer close, the invitation to join an exclusive club, "Why don't you join us on this one?" Some people respond to logic, others to emotion. There is no one magic close.

However, if you address the four issues above, either subtly or directly, in your close, you will be eminently more successful in closing. Your desired result is to get the client's business. The client's desired result is to receive value for moving business to you. That's it. It's that simple. You want the account, the client wants value. Show that if he or she does choose you, there is a high probability of getting to the desired result, that the cost is reasonable, and that the risk of disappointment is low. If you cover these three things, and these three things only, you will close a very high percentage of your prospects.

The Eight Steps to Successfully Closing Business

At the firm where I was introduced to high-powered selling techniques, they taught us how to close. We had one of the highest closing ratios in the business. For every four people we actually presented to face to face, we closed one, or 25 percent. Many of our prospects were people whom we had never met and who had never heard of our company. We weren't well known outside of a small circle of people on Wall Street. We didn't advertise, and we were a young company with no track record nor brand identity. Most people would have been happy with a 1 in 20 close ratio given those facts. We knew what we had to do in order to perform beyond the industry averages. We knew we had to do the following eight things:

1. See only highly qualified prospects

2. Get a face to face meeting

3. Deliver a high impact meeting and presentation

4. Show a demonstrably better knowledge of the business and product area

5. Keep a short sales cycle—roughly three months or less— usually less

6. Fill or kill often

7. Focus on risk control, not investment gains

8. Close fearlessly

In order to perform at levels most people only dream about, we developed a process and did not deviate. We studied our product specialties in depth. We knew more about the product area and the laws and tax issues surrounding it than the client's tax or legal advisors. There was nothing they could ask for which we didn't have the correct answer. We would role-play constantly. We tracked our results carefully. We closed fearlessly and regularly. The results were this: 24:1 meeting-to-close ratio. The highest per-man production on Wall Street for several years. The highest-paid sales force on Wall Street. Billions of equity dollars raised in a few short years.

In working with and interviewing the top producers in the financial sales business, I have learned that the following are "things that work." They don't work all the time, but I include them here because you may find one that helps you close a deal today or tomorrow.

Surrounding the Trade

I use a process I call "surrounding the trade" all the time for large-scale situations that involve major investment opportunities or large trades. Simply put, this is using strategic thinking and tactical awareness to close the client. You can look at it as closing off all other options so that the client really has the perception that there is only one proper, prudent, intelligent option left—and that is to do business with you. How do you do this?

You have to first know the competitive landscape. Who has the money now? Whom is he or she talking to about this situation? Who is he or she likely to talk to? Next, what are the client's real concerns and desires, beyond what is being said? Finally, know the outside influences. Is there anyone else involved in the decision? A CPA or attorney? Spouse, brother-in-law?

Start by writing each of the elements of the situation down in checklist format. Start checking off the list. Here's an example:

Situation: Large stock holding of family trust about to be liquidated. Patriarch is older and has turned many of the day to day details of the business over to his daughter and his son. The son runs the operations of the companies, and the daughter runs the finances. You are closer to the men in the family and always have been.

Step One: Get to know the daughter, and fast. Where does she come from philosophically on the topic of money? How does she view her role in the family? Who does she need and want to impress outside the family? How does she want to be perceived by her brother and others inside the family? Does she have an issue with men or with women?

This process revealed that the money is at the bank, she was a trained psychologist, saw her role as the protector of the family's assets, is smart but not financially sophisticated—though learning quickly. It's very important to her not to look stupid in business matters, particularly in front of her father and brother.

She doesn't particularly like men. Money is more of an intellectual exercise and challenge than anything else. It's important, but not for its ability to buy things like clothing or jewelry. It is important to her to be charitable and have a positive impact on issues that are close to her heart. Getting a good yield on their assets in a safe fashion is of primary importance; growth is a very far second. Competitively, she is looking at a stock that has a high yield—but isn't very well known, isn't very liquid—as an income and growth vehicle for this money.

She has asked our opinion of this stock as an investment. Like most truly wealthy people, the family has more money than they can ever spend . . . they just don't want to lose the asset base they've built. The family is very close to one particular bank in the community and is a large shareholder of the bank. Much of their liquid wealth is held there. But, we found out, the family isn't really comfortable with that given their shareholder status. They would prefer more privacy. Outside advisors do exist, but they aren't particularly well respected. The family has always relied on it's own common sense in making financial decisions, using outside CPA's and attorneys for answers to specific tax and legal questions.

Step Two: Strategy Checklist.

1. Identify number one and two buying issue for client

2. Identify other important issues

3. Neutralize outside advisors

4. Weaken opponents

5. Differentiate yourself

6. Attack the list

Here was our simple list:

Competitive

1. Bank has comparable products?

2. Outside advisor—potentially kill the deal? What reasons will he give?

3. Competing products under consideration. Advise the family.

Product Sale

1. Safety

2. Income

3. Proprietary nature—exclusivity

4. Liquidity

Emotional

1. Privacy—Assets held away from bank

2. Safety First—Income second.

What we did: Posing as potential customers, we called the bank and described our product and asked if they had anything like it we could invest in. They didn't. We called the family's other financial firms and did the same thing. There were some that were close, but none exactly like it. Ours was truly proprietary. We went through the exercise of role playing the outside advisor, coming up with every possible reason an outside advisor could come up with not to do the deal, and we developed responses.

We knew that we would never get the audience with the outside advisor but that we would possibly be able to hear his opinions and concerns by what questions the family asked us. We analyzed the other stock under consideration and gave a very clear presentation of the risks we saw there, risks that did not exist in our product. Also, our product had a much lower historical volatility than the stock they were considering, and it had a higher return. Our product had better liquidity characteristics. They would have serious impact costs both ways on a trade of the size they had in mind.

They hadn't even considered this element of the trade. We pointed out that the stock did seem to be that of a well-run company, but that if we were to advise one against the other, we would decisively go with our product. We also said that although we didn't see it today, there appeared to be risks there that we weren't comfortable with over and above those we could identify at this time. In essence, something smelled bad and we would advise the family to steer clear. We further stated that we couldn't be responsible for the performance of the other investment, so if they wanted to do that, they should do that elsewhere—we wouldn't take the order. Too many things bothered us, both identifiable and not so identifiable at this time.

We reiterated the true statistical nature of the performance of our product, the safety of the vehicles we invested in, and the proprietary nature of it. We further reminded them of the month-end closing. We guaranteed the privacy of the investment. For good measure, we made sure that one of our female team members interacted with the daughter, getting her into a discussion about her interests and causes outside the business. We closed the business. Time from meeting the client (for the first time) to closing: three weeks.

Create a Limited Availability for Your Services

Scarcity breeds desire. Tell the prospect in an appropriate manner that there are only so many people to whom you can deliver a high level of service. You would like very much to do business, but that soon you will have all the clients you can handle and that will be the end of it. This is true. It's like a successful mutual fund or hedge fund manager announcing he or she's going to close his fund. What happens when fund companies do this? The assets fly in. Do the same thing.

Ask for the Business—Then Shut Up!

This is an extremely important thing to learn in closing. Awkward silences are your friend. The old saying is, "He who speaks first, loses." Once you've asked for the business, shut up. Just *shut up*. Let the man think! Watch his face. See how he reacts. If you've done your job, he'll give you the business or he'll give you an objection.

Close and Move On

If you ask for the order and are rebuffed, traditional sales manuals tell you to "overcome the objection" and close again. If you have done the job right earlier in the sales process by creating the limited opportunity for them to work with you and showing them they have little risk in choosing you to manage their money or execute their transactions, you don't even have to close. They will ask you when you can get started. They will ask the closing question, "What do we have to do to get started?" This is the ideal case, and it doesn't always happen, because some people just want to hear you ask for the order—they like and respect someone who can ask for the business. So, don't disappoint them, go ahead and ask.

Keep the Prospect Off Balance

Throw trial closes at him when you're getting near. Stop in the middle of sentences and tell him you can see that he "gets it"—and just ask him if he's with you on that point, or if he agrees with you on the issue. Make sure the two of you are in sync. Then, when it feels like you should probably do a little more selling, *stop*. Ask for the business. Shut up, watch, and listen.

Ask for the Business—*Before* the Perfect Moment

If you wait until you're comfortable, you might never get around to asking for the business. I'm sure that there is the perfect closing moment. In fact, I may have experienced that moment a few times in my career, but it sure isn't because I consciously said to myself in the middle of a presentations, "Here it is . . . the perfect closing moment . . . Okay—Ready, *now!*" Assume there is no perfect closing moment. For all you know, this person had decided to give you the business before you even walked in the door. So waiting an hour to ask for the business may make you look silly. Start looking for the close the minute you walk in.

Fill or Kill Often

Don't let people string you along. You're a busy person. Very busy. You truly prefer to work hard on behalf of your existing clients. This person is a prospect, not a client. If the prospect wants to get the Rolls Royce treatment, he or she needs to be a client.

Focus on Risk Control

We can do things in the financial markets that control risk. These strategies, techniques, and individual instruments that limit or hedge against risk are valuable—we can execute them and lower the risk or volatility of a client's situation. We can't control the market movements, interest rates, world events . . . all things that have impact on the volatility of markets and economic life. So focusing on things you can control such as risk, with an eye for reasonable gains over time, will work for you and your clients.

To most people, risk of loss is their primary concern, particularly after rough or bear markets. They may want you to believe they are risk takers and courageous investors; however, the truth is nobody likes to lose the principal they have invested. They want to make money.

If you agree with this premise, then isn't it intelligent to address how you protect their principal first and generate a return on it second? The way we put it, "If we build a good solid foundation, we can go up as many stories as we want. But we absolutely have to protect the foundation. It has to be solid."

It's How You Say It

What sounds better? "Jim, here's the paperwork. There's a lot to fill out there, but it shouldn't take more than an hour. Would you like to open an account now?" Or, "Jim, I'm ready to go to work for you today, and I've had Melissa complete the paperwork for us . . . why don't you join us?" Be very careful in how you craft phrases and use words. Some phrases make people feel good, like they're joining a club; others are stark and cold.

There's a big difference between someone who says, "Let me bring in the guy from New York who does this for our firm" and, "With your permission, I'd like to deliver the person to you who has the best performance possible in this area. I'll have him in your office in the next few weeks, with your permission." Wouldn't you agree? Some people call them using power words. Words matter in our business. The key words here are "deliver" and "performance." The difference between these two statements is an obvious example. The first is a flat statement that hides the request for permission. The second one immediately defers to the client by asking permission outright. That shows tremendous respect. Beyond that, it hits subconscious positive psychological triggers with the words "deliver" and "performance." It's not that hard to do. It just takes practice and listening to what you say and thinking about how you could say it better. Asking someone in your office to role-play with you or just asking them which statements and questions sound better can be very helpful.

The way you speak can be just as influential to some as what you know. Pay attention to people's body language and facial expressions . . . and respond. I'm not asking you to change what it is that you have to say, but it's to your advantage to speak to people in the manner they prefer to be spoken to.

Allen, James. *As a Man Thinketh*. Putnam: New York, 1955.

Beck, Terry. *High Performance Selling*. HarperBusiness: Toronto, 2001.

Cialdini, Robert. *The Psychology of Persuasion*. Business Library: Melbourne, 1994.

Cleary, Thomas, tr. *The Art of War*. Sun Tsu. Shambhala: New York, 1991.

Davis, Gayle Ph.D. *High Performance Thinking for Business, Sports, and Life*. Psychology Connections: Colorado Springs, 1999.

Machowicz, Richard. *Unleashing the Warrior Within*. Hyperion: New York, 2000.

Peale, Norman Vincent. *The Power of Positive Thinking*. Simon & Schuster: New York, 1987.

Uzelac, Ellen. "Taking it to the Next Level," *Investment Adviser*, 2001.

A

Accountants, 132
Action, 40
Added value, 102
Advanced Fighter Weapons
  Training School, 1
Advisors, 132–34
Alliances, 127–29
American Express, 133–34
Appointments, 121
Assessment(s)
  of business/clients, 60–62
  of firm's "weapons," 62–68
  of results, 88–90
  of yourself, 59–60
Asset management fees, 84–86
Assets, under management, 70
Assumptions, 103
Attorneys, 132
Average efforts/results, 31, 54, 71

B

Baseball analogy, 3–4, 34–35, 115
Base year, 89
Basis points, 85
Beck, Michael, 144–35
Beck, Terry, 2–3
Belief, 40
Bloomberg, 74, 112
Bonds, convertible, 23
Book-ending technique, 146
Boston Consulting Group, 62
Boston Matrix, 62–65, 94
Broker sales programs, 129
Bryan, William Jennings, 1
Business owners, 108–11
Business structuring, 58–59
Buying, basic reasons for, 146–48

C

Capabilities, of firm, 72, 73–74
CARVER matrix, 118–20
Cash Cows, 64–65, 94
Casper, Garth, 91–92
Change, 14, 53, 147
Cialdini, Robert, 142–44
Clients
  assessing, 60–62
  minimum requirements for
    each, 76–77
  number of, reducing, 75–76,
    71, 75–76, 83–85
  productivity and, 74
  upgrading existing base of,
    77–84, 96–97
Closing strategies, 54, 159–71
  ask for the business, 167–69
  checklist, 164–65
  moving on, 168
  scarcity and, 167
  steps to success, 161–62
  surrounding the trade, 162–67
  value satisfaction and, 159–61
  verbal technique, 170–71
Cold calling, 112–14
Comfort zone, 14, 104
Competitive bids, 124–27
Compromise, 54, 150
Confidence, 47
Conrad, Mike, 107
Consistency, 18, 143
Convertible bonds, 23
Corporate officers, desires of, 154
Corporations, 111–12
Cosby, Bill, 21
Costs, 23–24
Currency, 95

D. Scott Kimball is a managing director for one of Wall Street's largest investment banks. He has spent twenty years on Wall Street, starting at E.F. Hutton while studying economics and political science at UCLA. He is the creator of a successful NYSE listed derivative, been involved in mergers and acquisitions, and currently manages long/short equity investments for private clients.

He is a member of the Association for Financial Professionals, the National Association for Business Economics, the American Economics Association, the National Association of Investment Professionals, and the Association for Investment Management Sales Executives. Prior to entering Wall Street, he was a professional baseball player with the Toronto Blue Jays Baseball Organization. He now resides in Atlanta, Georgia, with his family.

Create a Top Gun Team!

For special discounts on
20 or more copies of
Top Gun Financial Sales,
call Dearborn Trade Special Sales
at 800-621-9621, ext. 4455
or e-mail bermel@dearborn.com.
You'll receive great service
and top discounts.

For added visibility, please
consider our custom cover service,
which highlights your firm's name
and logo on the cover.
We are also an excellent resource
for dynamic and
knowledgeable speakers.

Dearborn™
Trade Publishing
A **Kaplan Professional** Company